STUDIES IN AMERICAN LITERATURE

Volume VII

☆☆☆☆☆☆☆☆☆☆☆☆☆☆☆☆☆☆☆☆☆☆☆☆☆☆☆☆☆☆☆☆☆☆

FORCE AND FAITH
IN THE NOVELS OF
WILLIAM FAULKNER

by

KENNETH E. RICHARDSON

Whitworth College – Spohane, Wash.

1967

MOUTON & CO.

THE HAGUE · PARIS

Printed in The Netherlands by Mouton & Co., Printers, The Hague.

FOR DOTTIE

who is my experience of grace

"*.... behold what manner of love the
Father hath bestowed upon us.*"

ACKNOWLEDGEMENTS

I would like to call attention to the fact that the writing and publication of this book was enhanced by gracious help from the following sources: Dr. Clarence J. Simpson looked at the manuscript in its early form and gave many helpful suggestions and encouragements. A generous grant from the Whitworth College Research Funds made publication possible. And the careful textual help given by Miss Joan Weathers eased the burden of creating accurate copy.

CONTENTS

CONTENTS

PROLOGUE – FORCE AND FAITH

As an acknowledged master of the American novel there is considerable interest in Faulkner's conception and use of faith. The novels of the last dozen years of his career are characterized by words like *belief, suffering, prevailing* plus the generous adoption of Christian symbols and myth. Of course, the chief example of such a book is his vast work *A Fable* on which he labored nine years and which was published with crosses on the cover signifying its spiritual nature. Despite the popular discovery of Faulkner's faith in "beliefs", it still does not seem that there exists a completely clear understanding of what faith means within his fiction, nor how faith is related to the other destructive or creative forces that make up his unique vision of human existence. Therefore, this book attempts to discover the relationship between the forces that operate in Faulkner's fictional world and what is now commonly referred to as "Faulkner's faith".

The only proper way to come to a clear understanding of Faulkner's concept of faith is to see it in relationship to his technique of opposing antithetical forces. This technique of polar opposition has been noted by critics and a variety of conclusions drawn from it. I would like to give a brief review of this critical opinion in order that I may more clearly show that the opposition of antithetical force in Faulkner's novels becomes a means for arriving at a concept of faith.

Faulkner scholarship looks back to 1939 and George Marion O'Donnell's essay, "Faulkner's Mythology", for a preliminary examination of dichotomous force in Faulkner.[1] O'Donnell ex-

[1] George Marion O'Donnell, "Faulkner's Mythology", in *Two Decades*

amined all thirteen of the Faulkner novels that had then been written (something not done before) and suggested that one principle bound his work together. Faulkner is a "traditional moralist in the best sense", he said: "One principle holds his thirteen books together. That principle is the Southern social-economic ethical tradition." The mythic structure of his work, O'Donnell felt, is built around the conflict between "traditionalism and the anti-traditional modern world in which it is immersed".[2] He divided Faulkner's world into two opposing camps and analyzed the thirteen novels to show the decay of the Compson-Sartoris tradition and the rise of Snopesism. To him the two groups did not represent persons as much as antithetical moral codes: thus he felt the struggle in Faulkner's novels was between humanism and naturalism. O'Donnell then attempted to interpret all the Faulkner novels from this point of view, and in so doing demonstrated the rewards of seeing Faulkner's work as a continuous whole, the nature of Faulkner's morality, and the antithetical structure in his fiction. However, the myth became somewhat strained when O'Donnell applied it to *Mosquitoes, As I Lay Dying* and *Sanctuary*. Subsequent Faulkner fiction has shown that the forces in operation and conflict in his fiction are more complex than O'Donnell thought.

The next important landmark in Faulkner criticism is Malcolm Cowley's introduction to *The Portable Faulkner* and Robert Penn Warren's review of Cowley.[3] Cowley explained the history of the Faulkner legend and showed that the Compsons and the Sartorises were inept in the conflict with the new and untraditional social order because of a "burden of conscience". He also pointed up the sharp structuring of conflict in Faulkner's fiction by way of antithetical arrangement. When Warren reviewed Cowley's introduction in *The New Republic* of August 12, 1946, he praised Cowley's work and once again opened the problem of antithesis

---

of Criticism, ed. Frederick Hoffman and Olga Vickery (East Lansing, 1954), pp. 49-62.

[2] *Ibid.*, p. 49.

[3] Malcolm Cowley, "Introduction to *The Portable Faulkner*", pp. 63-81, and Robert Penn Warren, "William Faulkner", pp. 82-101, both in *Two Decades of Criticism*.

in Faulkner: "To what extent", Warren asked, "does Faulkner work in terms of polarities, oppositions, paradoxes, inversions of roles? How much does he employ a line of concealed or open dialectic progression as a principle for his fiction?" [4] This, I believe, is one of the best questions asked about Faulkner's work, and this book is one answer to that question. Let me briefly illustrate role inversion as the means of dialectic progression: one force that is destructive in Faulkner's fiction is the trait of inflexibility, and this force is incarnate in the role of a rigid father. Conversely, one force that saves men is adaptability, and this force is dramatized in the figure of a spiritual father. Here is one arrangement of role inversion in Faulkner's novels that is repeated frequently enough to become the means of examining and ultimately advocating a principle of faith as a mode of life. I believe that the antithetical arrangement of destructive and creative force in Faulkner's novels is really a series of these role inversions involving man, woman, and society.

In the years following 1946 a number of other commentaries have appeared dealing with the subject of antithesis in Faulkner. The chief contributions to this line of investigation are Lawrance Thompson, "Mirror Analogues in *The Sound and the Fury*"; [5] Melvin Backman, "Sickness and Primitivism: A Dominant Pattern in William Faulkner's Work"; [6] Irving Malin's chapter on "The Technique of Oppositions"; [7] and Ward Miner's chapter on "Contrasts".[8] Other studies of the nature include Peter Swiggart's *The Art of Faulkner's Novels*, which is an analysis of the use of "primitives" and "puritans", and Walter Slatoff's *Quest for Failure: A Study of William Faulkner*.[9] Mr. Slatoff's book is of

[4]   *Ibid.*, p. 100.
[5]   Lawrance Thompson, "Mirror Analogues in *The Sound and the Fury*", in *English Institute Essays* (New York, 1952), pp. 83-106.
[6]   Melvin Backman, "Sickness and Primitivism: A Dominant Pattern in William Faulkner's Work", *Accent*, XIV (1954), pp. 61-73.
[7]   Irving Malin, *William Faulkner: An Interpretation* (Stanford, 1957), pp. 47-64.
[8]   Ward L. Miner, *The World of William Faulkner* (Chapel Hill, 1952), pp. 85-113.
[9]   Walter J. Slatoff, *Quest for Failure: A Study of William Faulkner* (Ithaca, 1960). Another recent study of interest is " 'The Bear', and Faulk-

particular interest because of the very thorough way he investigates patterned oppositions and the conclusions he draws from this technique.

Mr. Slatoff fails to see any connection between conceptual antithesis and dialectic progression in Faulkner. First of all he notes the tendency of the human mind to classify according to opposites.

All authors, and all human beings for that matter, tend very much to conceptualize life in broad polar or antithetic terms: black-white, right-wrong, heaven-hell, flesh-spirit, true-false, and the like. And I suppose that the major themes of any novel could be expressed antithetically. But even in this respect Faulkner goes beyond most; his works are unusual in the number, variety, and intensity even of major conceptual or thematic antitheses.[10]

He goes on to discuss many of these antitheses – motion and immobility, sound and silence, quiescence and turbulence, as well as character and stylistic antitheses. The major conceptual antitheses he sees are white-black, North-South, past-present, man-nature, natural-mechanical, modernism-primitivism, and words-action. After examining these antitheses in terms of their occurrence within each novel, Slatoff says that different antitheses operate at different times and that several may operate simultaneously and more or less independently.[11] My study supports Slatoff's concept of antithetical arrangement in Faulkner, even though my belief in the meaning of the antitheses differs from his.

The use I make of oppositions in setting up and describing destructive and creative force in Faulkner is twofold. First of all, I

---

ner's Moral Vision", *Studies in Faulkner* (Pittsburgh, 1961), by Neal Woodruff, Jr. Woodruff feels Faulkner's moral vision is exemplified by "four broad types of character that reappear frequently throughout Faulkner's works – the victim, the self-enslaved, the exploiter, and the self-contained" (p. 60). He sees that Faulkner expresses his forces in antithetical character types. What I call the troubled son he calls the victim, inflexible fathers are roughly analogous to the self-enslaved, the exploiters are the Snopes, the self-contained are the creative men in motion. One great omission in Woodruff's short study is a consideration of Faulkner's women.
[10] *Ibid.*, p. 88.
[11] *Ibid.*, p. 106.

attempt to identify the forces of destruction; these I find to be patriarchal inflexibility, sexual irresponsibility, and Snopesism. These forces encounter resistance or opposition (dramatic conflict) from the people or groups they threaten. Thus the father representing inflexibility is in opposition to the son; the carnal female is in opposition to a husband, brother, or son; and the amoral Snopes threaten the social solidarity of the community. In turn these destructive forces are opposed by creative forces: the wilderness father, mother love, and social morality. Slatoff has labelled the artistic talent that expresses itself in this fashion as "the polar imagination", and he means by this designation the "deep-seated tendency in Faulkner to view and interpret experience in extreme terms and to see life as composed essentially of pairs of warring entities".[12] Slatoff points out the unresolved tensions that exist *within* Faulkner's novels and suggests that Faulkner's desire to leave them unresolved is really "a quest for failure". My approach is somewhat different: I consider the polar imagination of Faulkner's work as a whole, and I reach a different conclusion from Slatoff. In some novels there are unresolved tensions, and where this is the case, the result is generally tragic, and the force in operation (i.e., the source of the tension) is destructive. In other novels certain characters have resolved personal tensions and bring a creative and renewing power to the social situation. The pattern of the forces suggests that through the body of Faulkner's fiction there is a progressive resolution of tension which finally ends up as a positive view where *all* tensions may be resolved by creative force. *A Fable* and *The Mansion*, the most ambitious and the most significant works of his last period, illustrate the latest Faulkner view. The patterned opposition of force in Faulkner's novels is, therefore, not a quest for failure at all but what Warren originally suggested it might be: "a line of concealed (or open) dialectic progression",[13] and I believe this progression is a quest for a faith that may act as a governing principle of human behavior.

This study is arranged in the following way: there are three

[12] *Ibid.*, p. 79.
[13] Warren, in *Two Decades of Criticism*, p. 100.

large divisions entitled "Man", "Woman", and "Society". In each of these categories I discuss a destructive and a creative force. These forces operate in Faulkner's tragic world and in his enduring and prevailing world. In the chapter "Faith and the World", I attempt to illustrate how Faulkner's recent fiction is characterized by the resolution of destructive and creative antitheses in favor of prevailing faith. The epilogue is a summary of the meaning of faith and the effects its emergence has created in Faulkner's novels.

MAN

I. SOCIETY AND THE INFLEXIBLE FATHER

> You see, I had a design in my mind.
> Whether it was a good or a bad de-
> sign is beside the point.
>
> *Absalom, Absalom!* [1]

The late Clyde Kluckhohn once noted that in the American way of life "the son must 'go farther' than his father, and revolt against the father in adolescence is expected".[2] This observation illuminates two elements within the American dream: the ideal of success and the expectation of challenge. In Faulkner's work there is a repeated use of the father-son relationship; he sees the father as a representative of a social *status quo* and the son's revolt as a test of the existing social pattern. The tension between the father and the son destroys the filial relationship and "the father [be-comes] the natural enemy of any son and son-in-law",[3] because the son's urge to go farther than his father is the result of an inborn human characteristic. Just as the son must test the social pattern, just so must the father protect and maintain it. "Society must obviously have patterns of behavior", observes S. A. Hayakawa; "human beings must obviously have habits. But when those pat-terns become inflexible . . . such a [society] is headed for trouble. There is insufficient capacity for differentiated behavior." [4] The

[1] *Absalom, Absalom!*, p. 263. A complete list of Faulkner's novels ap-pears as the first page of the bibliography. Throughout the notes only the novels and page number will be given.
[2] Clyde Kluckhohn, *Mirror for Man* (New York, 1949), p. 234.
[3] *Absalom, Absalom!*, p. 104.
[4] S. A. Hayakawa, "Reactions and Words", written especially for *A Com-plete Course in Freshman English*, ed. Harry Shaw (New York, 1958), p. 266.

trouble within Faulkner's fiction is an inflexible father who protects a habitual pattern of behavior by erecting a tightly designed
way of life which he seeks to impose upon society in the person of
his son. His insufficient capacity for differentiated responses is an
index of an unwillingness to change or tolerate revolt. The result
is a destructive pattern that is repeated within all of the great
Faulkner novels.

I would like to examine this pattern in Faulkner's fiction
chronologically beginning with *Sartoris* and developing it through
The Sound and the Fury and *Absalom, Absalom!* The pattern is
most complex in *Light in August*. By examining the fathers and
sons in each of these novels and the pattern of family and social
relationships they exhibit, we can see (1) the inflexible nature
of the father's personality, (2) the nature of the father's protective design or dream, (3) the nature of the social structure the
father fights to preserve and (4) the nature and meaning of the
son's revolt.

Sartoris, which introduces the Yoknapatawpha legend, tells
how the Sartoris family romanticize the glamorous deeds of
Colonel John Sartoris and his son Bayard before and during the
Civil War. The family legend dictates a specific type of character
and action for all of the male Sartorises. Each male descendant is
expected to be as powerful, gallant, reckless, and violent as his
forefathers. For instance, Colonel John Sartoris helped found
Jefferson, and his behavior at that time defines a way of life in
which power is a goal and daring behavior a symbol of the worthiness to possess it. Bayard Sartoris is killed while undertaking a
valiant and reckless charge at the battle of Manassas in order to
capture a jar of anchovies. In time the actions of such men achieve
epic proportions and splendor; in time the story of their way of
life achieves the power of myth. The central theme of *Sartoris* is
the struggle of young Bayard Sartoris, a veteran of World War I,
to understand and live with the inflexible myth.

The actual facts of Sartoris history have been separated from
mere history by Aunt Jenny Du Pre and the village historian, old
man Falls. Aunt Jenny is the one who introduces Bayard and his
brother Johnny to the Sartoris tradition:

It was she who told them of the manner of Bayard Sartoris' death prior to the second battle of Manassas. She had told the story many times since . . . and as she grew older the tale itself grew richer and richer, taking on a mellow splendor like wine; until what had been a harebrained prank of two heedless and reckless boys wild with their own youth had become a gallant and finely tragical focal point to which the history of the race had been raised from out the old miasmic swamps of spiritual sloth by two angels valiantly fallen and strayed, altering the course of human events and purging the souls of men.

Old man Falls adds to the heroic significance of Sartoris action by glorifying the Sartorises as village representatives. Thus the dream of Colonel John Sartoris, the quest for power and the need for violent action and the glamor it brings, is refined by these two storytellers until it becomes a "gallant and finely tragical focal point" [5] for the two remaining descendants, Bayard and Johnny. What Faulkner wishes to show, however, is that the dream originated in calculated foolishness and dare-devil egotism. Thus he calls Colonel John Sartoris "the virus, the inspiration and example . . . which dominated them all".[6] And his inflexibility is reflected in his desire to "stiffen and shape that which sprang from him into the fatal semblance of his dream".[7] The latent destructive power of John Sartoris' dream is pointed out by Olga Vickery:

In its effect however, the dream becomes progressively more destructive as it takes on all the force of a categorical imperative for Colonel John Sartoris' descendants. Spontaneous reactions to experience are replaced by imitative rituals in which form becomes more important than meaning. The final result is apt to be either an outbreak of violence or complete paralysis. At its most extreme, devotion to the dead and their design can mean a complete denial of one's own life.[8]

Young Bayard Sartoris soon discovers that he is expected to fulfill the legend and the design of his great grandfather, but he seems to lack the power to do this. He will not admit this to himself, however, and he refuses to judge and condemn the validity of the

[5] *Sartoris*, p. 9.
[6] *Ibid.*, p. 375.
[7] *Ibid.*, p. 23.
[8] Olga W. Vickery, *The Novels of William Faulkner* (New Orleans, 1959), p. 19.

Sartoris dream. Therefore, he is caught in an insoluble dilemma.

It is a war experience with his brother that shows Bayard he does not naturally possess the temperament to fulfill the Sartoris tradition. He and his brother John are American aviators on duty in France. When they are attacked by the Germans and Johnny is hit, he reacts with typical Sartoris recklessness: "Then he thumbed his nose at me like he was always doing and flipped his hand at the Hun and kicked his machine out of the way and jumped." [9] Bayard's reaction, however, lacks color and glamor; he is terrified and feels a surging desire to save himself.

Momentarily, the world was laid away and he was a trapped beast in the high blue, mad for life, trapped in the very cunning fabric that had betrayed him who had dared chance too much.[10]

Consequently, he turns his plane away from the conflict and returns to his base. When Bayard returns home, he is conscience-stricken at his desertion of Johnny, and he determines to come to terms with the Sartoris legend of reckless daring. He erects an inflexible pattern of behavior for himself that is a protest against the Sartoris legend even while it is a fulfillment. Bayard's design is self-destructive, however, because he forces himself into unnatural behavior and slowly loses all human responsiveness.

When Bayard starts to live dangerously, his actions begin to exhibit his death wish. He loses his spontaneous warmth and becomes a man "without any affection for anything at all"; his eyes reflect a "terror ... and a mad cold fury and despair".[11] Soon after, he marries, and it is only a little while before his wife senses an air of self-induced fatality about him.

She took his face between her palms and drew it down, but his lips were cold and upon them she tasted fatality and doom ... And they would lie so, holding to one another in the darkness and the temporary abeyance of his despair and the isolation of that doom he could not escape.

Bayard's search for meaningful life through violence causes his wife to realize "as she never had before the blind tragedy of

[9] *Sartoris*, p. 252.
[10] *Ibid.*, p. 203.
[11] *Ibid.*, p. 250.

human events". Despite the fact that he becomes acutely aware of danger, he soon is in despair over the long empty prospect of life: "Nothing to be seen, and the long, long span of a man's natural life." Bayard comes to feel all of life is "gray beneath the season of dissolution and death".[12] Eventually he finds the escape he desires by knowingly testing a faulty airplane. He does not fulfill the pattern of Sartoris violence; he commits suicide to escape it.

The imposition of a design of the past upon the present is really a projection of an old dead pattern upon people who are pawns. In one of his most romantically styled passages, Faulkner expresses the fatal quality of such a situation by associating the tragedy of the Sartorises with *The Song of Roland*.

The music went on in the dusk softly; the dusk was peopled with ghosts of glamorous and old disastrous things. And if they were just glamorous enough, there was sure to be a Sartoris in them, and then they were sure to be disastrous. Pawns. But the Player, and the game He plays ... He must have a name for His pawns, though. But perhaps Sartoris is the game itself – a game outmoded and played with pawns shaped too late and to an old dead pattern, and of which the Player Himself is a little wearied. For there is death in the sound of it, and a glamorous fatality, like silver pennons downrushing at sunset, or a dying fall of horns along the road to Roncevaux.[13]

Bayard Sartoris is a pawn, and the novel shows us that the Sartoris family myth is an old dead pattern. Bayard engages in a fatal game of death where he does not know the rules because they were formulated by the dreams of his ancestors. His silent struggle within the Sartoris design is like the dying fall of Roland's horn – a call for help that comes too late because of pride.

Yet the essential intent of *Sartoris* is to show Bayard Sartoris as a victim. He is controlled by an inflexible family tradition and his own revolt. The myth of the Sartoris family dominates him, for he feels the need to respond in some way to the obligations thrust upon him by his ancestors; however, by nature he simply does not react to glamorous disaster as self-realization. His per-

[12] *Ibid.*, p. 289.
[13] *Ibid.*, p. 380.

sonal revolt against the legend controls him because he can conceive of only one response to violence: a counter-violence. Therefore, like all of the Sartorises, he moves "romantically, finely, and a little tragically" [14] within a restrictive environment. Ironically enough, the very violence with which he seeks escape perpetuates the legend he is unable to fulfill. *Sartoris* is tragic in its implications because Bayard is a victim of the personal inflexibility of his great grandfather, Col. John Sartoris, and the social system that accepts and perpetuates the dead man's fatal dream.

The figure of an inflexible father, introduced in Sartoris, is carried forward in *The Sound and the Fury*. It is somewhat surprising that so few critics have examined Quentin Compson's actions in relation to the influence of his father and mother upon him. Almost everyone wants to see his problem in terms of his relationship to Caddy, yet there is no doubt that she is but a symbol of the family to him. Her loss of chastity represents a loss of family honor; his claim of incest with her is nothing more than the substitution of a more horrible symbol with the hope it will redeem and reclaim her sin for the family; then, he hopes, it will be "the two of us amid the pointing and the horror". The strongest intellectual influence upon Quentin is his father – he is his mentor; and the strongest emotional influence upon him is his mother. When he was at the University of Virginia, Faulkner was asked about Quentin's relationship to his father.

Q.: Mr. Faulkner, I'd like to ask you about Quentin and his relationship with his father. I think many readers get the impression that Quentin is the way he is to a large extent because of his father's lack of values, or the fact that he doesn't seem to pass down to his son many values that will sustain him. Do you think Quentin winds up the way he does primarily because of that . . .? [15]

Mr. Faulkner's direct answer was "the action as portrayed by Quentin was transmitted to him through his father". He went on to explain that perhaps Quentin's problem is a long line of inflexible ancestors, suggesting again the theme we have already

---

[14]   *Ibid.*, p. 194.
[15]   Frederick Gwynn and Joseph Blotner, *Faulkner in the University* (Charlottesville, 1959), pp. 2-3.

seen in *Sartoris:* a son trapped by an inflexible design erected by
his forefathers. Quentin's response to his father's inflexibility is
the same as that of Bayard Sartoris. He is forced into a compulsive
counter-design. Quentin builds an order of his own that is as rigid
as any. "The cause of his ineffectuality and his ultimate destruction", says Mrs. Vickery, "is the fact that his system antecedes
his experience and eventually is held in defiance of experience".[16]
I believe that the failure to interpret Quentin in relation to his
father can mislead one in the estimation of his character. For instance, Irving Howe finds Quentin to be a Hamlet-like figure
"too weak, too passive, too bewildered for the role of sensitive
hero".[17] Melvin Backman echoes this idea in referring to all of the
troubled sons in Faulkner's fiction as "sick, young heroes".[18]
However, Quentin's weakness, passivity, and bewilderment must
be seen in terms of his father's and mother's influence upon him.
The novel demands that one interpret the story as the tragic record of a family, the last of a princely line.[19]

Mr. Compson's life is a calculated retreat from responsibility.
At one time he entertained notions of being governor, but he could
never effectively get engaged in politics because he could never
believe that anything like that could really matter. Like Miniver
Cheevy he feels the days of greatness are past, and, also like
Miniver, he keeps on drinking. His wife and his brother-in-law
are something like private jokes to him. He regards their weakness
and foolishness as adequate proof of man's nature; his daughter is
just another woman – instinctively female, therefore, instinctively selfish. And the idiocy, idealism, and meanness of his three
sons mirror to him the imperfections that make the human situation preposterous. Since he inherited the Compson property and
the last of its wealth, he can afford to retreat to his private, down-
town office where he can sit "all day long with a decanter of
whiskey and a litter of dogeared Horaces and Livys and Catulluses
composing ... caustic and satiric eulogies on both his dead and

16 Vickery, *The Novels of William Faulkner*, p. 37.
17 Irving Howe, *William Faulkner: A Critical Study* (New York, 1951),
p. 119.
18 Backman, "Sickness and Primitivism", p. 61.
19 Gwynn and Blotner, *Faulkner in the University*, p. 3.

his living fellowtownsmen".[20] His typical way is to dismiss the significance of the human situation with words, and the nominal world is his tool as well as his reality. He employs words to mock his family as well as the meaning of life itself. Quentin becomes his principal audience, and the father uses his son's devotion and credulity as a means of verifying the validity of his thoughts. "The horror of the situation", as Irving Malin points out,

> is that Mr. Compson discovers delight in transmitting his design, born of fear and despair, to his adolescent son. His delight is not so much in fiendishness as it is in pride. In spite of his emphasis upon man's insignificance he feels inwardly that he is better than most men, for he has seen the meaning of life in a clear way. He is proud to give his son, Quentin, his knowledge, which will, he feels, help him to live properly according to the authoritarianism he himself has adopted.[21]

Quentin feels the destructive impact of his father's beliefs because his father is the one logical source of information and meaning for his life. The son's problem is centered in his family and specifically the relationship of his sister's promiscuity to the whole family honor. No one else knows this situation as does his father, and there is no one else in the family to whom Quentin goes for explanation. He feels his mother is completely wrapped up in herself; his sister is selfishly sexual and unable to explain or express herself; one of his brothers is an idiot, and the other is a boor. Quentin fights against accepting his father's despair, and he does argue with him continually, but he never comes up with a set of beliefs of his own that differ from his father's. All that he can do is erect a design (the claim of incest) as unreal as his father's. It must be remembered, too, that Quentin is involved in a patriarchal situation in his Southern home. It is natural for him to look to his father, since his father directs the family affairs in accordance with a long line of Compson tradition. He cannot go outside of his family to solve his problems because that would necessitate the revelation of his sister's character and behavior. Therefore, Quentin keeps his search for meaning private and depends entirely upon his father for guidance.

[20] *The Sound and the Fury*, p. 8.
[21] Malin, *William Faulkner*, p. 17.

Through ridicule and satire Mr. Compson destroys all hope in his son. On the day of his suicide Quentin recalls a number of different remarks made to him by his father. The first thought on that day is stimulated by hearing the ticking of his grandfather's watch as he lies in bed. He thinks:

When Father gave it to me he said, Quentin, I give you the mauso-leum of all hope and desire; it's rather excruciating-ly [sic] apt that you will use it to gain the reducto absurdum of all human experience which can fit your individual needs no better than it fitted his or his father's. I give it to you not that you may remember time, but that you might forget it now and then for a moment and not spend all your breath trying to conquer it. Because no battle is ever won he said. They are not even fought. The field only reveals to man his own folly and despair, and victory is an illusion of philosophers and fools.[22]

This defeatist attitude is repeated time and again by Mr. Compson; human experience is absurd, he feels, because there is no ultimate meaning. He expresses this explicitly to his son when Quentin is trying to find a way of understanding and accepting his sister's loss of chastity, and Quentin is thereby robbed of seeing a meaning in either sin or holiness.

He said it was men invented virginity not women. Father said it's like death: only a state in which the others are left and I said, But to believe it doesn't matter and he said, That's what's so sad about any-thing: not only virginity, and I said, Why couldn't it have been me and not her who is unvirgin and he said, That's why that's sad too; nothing is even worth the changing of it.[23]

Later in the day Quentin remembers a statement his father made that man is fully defined now and hereafter by the folly and trage-dy of being born.

Father said a man is the sum of his misfortunes. One day you'd think misfortune would get tired, but then time is your misfortune Father said. A gull on an invisible wire attached through space dragged. You carry the symbol of your frustration into eternity. Then the wings are bigger Father said, only who can play a harp.[24]

The sum of Mr. Compson's teaching is that men are like flies

---

[22] *The Sound and the Fury*, p. 95.
[23] *Ibid.*, p. 97.
[24] *Ibid.*, p. 123.

whom the gods kill for their sport. In fact, as Quentin sees, he taught all of his children a philosophy of despair.

Father was teaching us that all men are just accumulations dolls stuffed with sawdust swept up from the trash heaps where all previous dolls had been thrown away the sawdust flowing from what wound in what side that not for me died not.[25]

There is no possibility of salvation or redemption in Mr. Compson's mind. Christ, he feels, "was not crucified; he was worn away by a minute clicking of little wheels".[26] The father blocks off every avenue of escape from hopelessness through a solipsistic unbelief.

Mr. Compson's fatalism makes him inflexible. Quentin cannot escape the tragic consequences of his father's view of life nor his influence, as his suicide clearly indicates. The father's design of life is powerful and unvarying. He never breaks, never leaves an opening for hope, never suggests there may be an alternative; he only intensifies his expressions of hopelessness. The tight little fortress of his life is impregnable because he does not need or want anybody. He is unwilling to act humanely or even act at all because to act is to risk something of himself. And he has none of himself to give away or share. Mr. Compson will never become engaged with life, personality, or faith, because he is unsure of the response he will get. He is unwilling, as Robert Penn Warren observes, to act in the human situation, unwilling to take the risk of his humanity.[27] He would rather lose by default than take a chance. A man risks something only when he has faith; to Mr. Compson faith is impossible because God is "a dark diceman" who has already loaded the dice against man, and man's "despair or remorse or bereavement is not particularly important to the dark diceman".[28] Without the flexibility supplied by faith or humanity he cannot become a "man in motion" – Faulkner's ideal of flexibility and humane responsiveness. He is a father who

[25] *Ibid.*, p. 194.
[26] *Ibid.*, p. 96.
[27] Robert Penn Warren, "Cowley's Faulkner", *New Republic*, CXV (August 12, 1946), pp. 176-180.
[28] *The Sound and the Fury*, p. 196.

gives his son a stone when he asks for bread, gives a serpent when
he asks for a fish. All that Quentin can gain from his father is
despair. Quentin does not possess Nietzsche's power to look into
the abyss of meaninglessness and fly over with the wings of an
eagle. Therefore, the sound and the fury in Quentin's mind is but
the echo of his father's vain philosophy.

The title of *Absalom, Absalom!* indicates that once again
Faulkner is dealing with a father-son relationship. David's lament
for his dead son, "O my son Absalom, my son, my son Absalom!
would God I had died for thee",[29] is a classic expression of paternal grief. The title of Faulkner's novel is ironic, however, for the
grief that Thomas Sutpen should feel for the death of his sons is
lacking. He has no lament because all of his paternal feeling is
swallowed up in his "design" which is "to gain individual recognition through material conformity".[30] This novel broadens the
theme of inflexibility, for Faulkner makes very clear that "Sutpen's personal compulsions are an important parallel to the social
order"[31] of the South. And when Sutpen attempts to make his
sons accept his design in order to perpetuate his desire for individual recognition, he not only acts as the representative of an
established social system, he acts as a law-giver who dramatically
illustrates the destructive animosity of a "father who is the
natural enemy of any son and son-in-law".[32]

When Sutpen's life is just about over, he summarizes all of his
experience with the words "You see, I had a design in my mind.
Whether it was a good or a bad design is beside the point."[33]
What he now wishes to find out is what went wrong with it, where
it erred, in order that he may correct the flaw and once again feel
the security of a tightly patterned way of life. From the time he
is fourteen years old Sutpen pursues his fantastic dream, even to
the moment of death. The grim strength of his will is the equivalent of the remorseless inhumanity of his rigid plan. As we examine *Absalom, Absalom!* we look to see the inception of Sut-

[29] II Samuel 18 : 33.
[30] Malin, *William Faulkner*, p. 5.
[31] *Ibid.*, p. 6.
[32] *Absalom, Absalom!*, p. 104.
[33] *Ibid.*, p. 263.

pen's design and its effect upon his character, and the destructive power of his inflexible personality upon his sons.

In 1820 when Thomas Sutpen is a boy of fourteen, his family come down out of their mountain home and discover the rest of Southern society. The mountain people had stressed the fundamental human values of brotherhood and communal living – "Because where he lived the land belonged to anybody and everybody and so the man who would go to the trouble and work to fence off a piece of it and say, 'This is mine' was crazy." In the valley below, however, the Sutpen family find the land is "all divided and fixed and neat with a people living on it all divided and fixed and neat because of what color their skins happened to be and what they happened to own".[34] Here the Negro and poverty represent inferiority. When Sutpen is sent on an errand to a large plantation house, he is turned away from the door by a "monkey-nigger". Nothing has ever prepared him for such a response, and Sutpen's pride is mortally wounded. He creeps away to a cave where he figures "he would have to do something about it in order to live with himself for the rest of his life".[35] In the cave he dedicates the rest of his life to vindicate that little boy at the door, what he himself calls the "boy symbol". He has already discovered his weapon in the pattern of life existent in the valley: "So to combat them you have got to have what they have that made them do what the man did. You got to have land and niggers and a fine house to combat them with." [36] In an instant Sutpen has cast his plan and exchanged individual integrity for social convention, and he makes this exchange even though he instinctively feels the behavior of the plantation owner as expressed through the Negro is wrong. Through deliberate choice Sutpen becomes an image of the South; he exchanges his mountain ethics for a corrupt measure of man in which the Negro is used for purely selfish purposes.

Sutpen becomes possessed by his plan to achieve power and, as he succeeds, he begins to lose human and moral characteristics.

[34] *Ibid.*, p. 221.
[35] *Ibid.*, p. 234.
[36] *Ibid.*, p. 238.

Other people begin to see him as a demon, a monster, a devil, for he is pushed by "a gaunt and tireless driving – a quiet and unflagging fury".[37] He becomes, Faulkner says, "completely the slave of his secret and furious impatience".[38] People fear him, because they realize that this man is ruthless, without pity or love, and will do anything to fulfill his plan for life. Mr. Compson suggests that these negative qualities are really testimonies to Sutpen's "innocence".

Sutpen's trouble was innocence. All of a sudden he discovered, not what he wanted to do but what he just had to do, had to do it whether he wanted to or not, because if he did not do it he knew that he could never live with himself for the rest of his life, . . . with all the dead ones waiting and watching to see if he was going to do it right.[39]

That is, Sutpen is no longer a master in the South; he too is a slave faithfully and innocently representing through his life the values of a society he has adopted as his own. Mrs. Vickery summarizes the relationship between Sutpen's character and his "innocence" in this way:

Sutpen's "innocence" is manifest: it consists not only of his unquestioning belief in the value of all the idols of the South but in his belief that the structure, the design, is itself the secret of its strength and its perpetuation, that he need only follow its ritual to grasp its substance and that he can do so with the same blunt honesty which was a part of his mountain heritage.[40]

The design actually replaces Sutpen's sense of morality. He comes to believe that "the ingredients of morality [are] like the ingredients of pie or cake".[41] This materialistic approach will not function in a purely human world, so Sutpen seeks to "hold clear and free above a maelstrom of unpredictable and unreasoning human beings . . . his code of logic and morality, his formula and recipe of fact and deduction". But his divorce from humanity is so great that the "balanced sum and product [of his logic and morality]

---

[37] Ibid., pp. 36, 42.
[38] Ibid., p. 34.
[39] Ibid., p. 220.
[40] Vickery, The Novels of William Faulkner, p. 95.
[41] Absalom, Absalom!, p. 263.

declined, refused to swim or even float".[42] Sutpen's "innocence" therefore, is really evidence of his inhumanity and amorality because good and evil do not even exist for him. When something goes wrong, it is a "scientific" mistake he searches for – like a miscalculation in a column of figures. And that, of course, is Sutpen's evil – he treats people as things. As Hyatt Waggoner points out, Sutpen never becomes aware, in Martin Buber's terminology, of an I-thou relationship; it is always I-it.

Sutpen was the new man, the post-Machiavellian man consciously living by power-knowledge alone, refusing to acknowledge the validity of the principles that he cannot or will not live by and granting reality to nothing that cannot be known with abstract rational clarity. He lives by a calculated expediency.[43]

There is a keen point to Shreve's description of Sutpen as Faustus, but he is also like Milton's Satan, Captain Ahab, and Ethan Brand. In Southern terms he is a monomaniacal careerist emptied of all humanity. In human terms he is the father-type created by artificial insemination.

It is Sutpen's two sons, Charles Bon and Henry, who suffer most from the pressures of their father's inflexible personality and design. Charles Bon needs his father's recognition ("that instant of indisputable recognition") in order to have any meaning for this life. Sutpen absolutely refuses to admit Bon is his son because he is part Negro – a condition in Bon's mother that Sutpen is unaware of when he marries her. As soon as he discovers his wife and child possess Negro blood he calmly puts them aside with a cash settlement. He knows their mixed blood is a threat to the social rigidity of the races, which he depends upon to achieve a feeling of superiority. Bon, however, comes to his father's plantation, and the boy symbol is repeated. His unspoken demand for recognition is denied, just as it was to the father, for the sake of the design. But Bon refuses to accept the *status quo*; he revolts against the father's design in order to gain recognition. Bon conceives of a plan of his own. By threatening to marry Judith, Sut-

---

[42]   *Ibid.*, p. 275.
[43]   Hyatt Waggoner, *William Faulkner: From Jefferson to the World* (Lexington, Kentucky, 1959), p. 166.

pen's only daughter, he feels he can force his father to recognize him.

> That's all I want. He need not even acknowledge me; I will let him understand just as quickly that he need not do that, that I do not expect that, will not be hurt by that, just as he will let me know that quickly that I am his son.[44]

Sutpen maintains his silence; he cannot act spontaneously; he cannot act humanely. Bon has become a threat that must be handled by the design itself, so Sutpen employs his second son to protect the family and their way of life. O'Connor regards Bon's situation as a Southern tragedy, but it is more than that – "it is the tragedy of the son whose father refuses him his proper and needed recognition and acceptance. In our modern idiom, it is called the search for a father".[45]

When Henry Sutpen learns from his father that his college friend Charles Bon is his half-brother and part Negro, he is, of course, amazed. But when he also discovers that Bon is planning to marry his sister in order to force a recognition from their father, he is convinced of the course of action that must be pursued. Bon must be stopped for one reason – miscegenation. Henry supports the social pattern of his region which regards mixed blood with horror because it is a threat to social rigidity in future ages. The father puts upon Henry the burden of preventing Bon from marrying Judith, and Henry is torn by two conflicting loyalties: obedience to his father and the social system of his region, and a love for his friend and brother. The showdown comes at the close of the Civil War. All of the Sutpens have been valiantly fighting to protect and preserve the Southern way of life. Even Bon has fought for the South in order to be near his father. As the war draws to a close, Bon makes known to Henry that he plans to return and marry their sister. He knows that their father has put the responsibility upon Henry to stop this, so he tests his brother to see whether brother-love, the fear of incest, or the fear of miscegenation is the strongest. Henry can bear the thought of

[44] *Absalom, Absalom!*, p. 319.
[45] William Van O'Connor, *The Tangled Fire of William Faulkner* (Minneapolis, 1954), p. 95.

incest; when Bon says, "So it's the miscegenation, not the incest, which you can't bear. Henry doesn't answer." When Bon invites Henry to kill him, right then, all Henry can say is, "You are my brother." Bon responds, "No I'm not. I'm the nigger that's going to sleep with your sister. Unless you stop me Henry." [46] But Henry Sutpen cannot stop his brother right then. He follows him all the way back to the plantation, struggling within himself to discover what he must do. When Bon enters the plantation gates, he shoots him. This act clearly reveals the power of his father's dream; it also reveals that the social system of the South is stronger in Henry than the love of a brother and the fear of murder. As one observer notes, "The scene of the murder of Bon by Henry after he has learned that the other is part black is a significant archetypal situation in Southern history." [47] Henry has reenacted the violence that helped establish the design of slavery and demonstrated the extent to which a man will go to protect a way of life. His action, as William Poirier points out, is a "terribly difficult moral act. It had to be carried out in a world which his father, like Quentin's mother in *The Sound and the Fury,* has almost wholly corrupted. Henry acts not in obedience to his father, but to an inherent sense of a moral code which is stronger than his love for Bon." [48] Charles Bon and Henry Sutpen are seeking to find a personal meaning for their lives; as Frederick J. Hoffman points out, "the sons want something other than abstract power; and, in looking beyond it, they upset [the father's] drive for power." [49] It is, however, this drive for power, this vaulting ambition of Thomas Sutpen's, that is the overpowering influence, making these sons live in terms of the father's selfish will. Consequently, the tragic patterns of behavior the father forces upon his sons are what lead Henry to the final judgment of the father and the novel: "He . . . has destroyed us all." [50]

[46] *Absalom, Absalom!,* pp. 356-58.
[47] Malin, *William Faulkner,* p. 8.
[48] William Poirier, "Strange Gods in Jefferson: Analysis of *Absalom, Absalom!*", in *William Faulkner: Two Decades of Criticism,* ed. Frederick T. Hoffman and Olga Vickery (East Lansing, 1954), p. 240.
[49] Frederick J. Hoffman, *William Faulkner* (New Haven, 1961), p. 76.
[50] *Absalom, Absalom!,* p. 334.

When this novel is considered as a whole, Mr. Compson's perspective is somewhat helpful; he regards the tragedy of Sutpen a punishment of *hubris* in the manner of the Greek tragic hero who is struck down for his arrogance. As Ilse Dusoir Lind says, the novel is a "grand tragic vision of historic dimension" in which "the hero falls because of an innate deficiency of moral insight". And since Sutpen's error is also a social one, his life becomes a "representative anecdote" of the tragic human failure of the father.[51]

The design is a symbol of pathological compulsion. However, Faulkner's interest in the human situation extends beyond the individual pathologically fixed on self-fulfillment; he relates "the pattern of compulsion . . . to his own environment as a Southerner. . . . His own region, he believes, is grounded upon ideals as abstract and inhuman as the personal design." [52] *Light in August* is that novel which attempts to illustrate the contemporary social implications of the desire for rigidity. Richard Chase notes that in this novel "Faulkner seems to be concerned with showing that the codes modern man *does* set up do *not* allow him to define himself as human – that codes have become compulsive patterns which man clings to in fear and trembling while the pattern emasculates him." [53] The son of man in the story, Joe Christmas, is pictured as the victim of three inflexible father-types, each of whom represents an aspect of life and society: his grandfather, his foster father, and a figure I would somewhat ironically refer to as a godfather. Joe Christmas is really modern man trying to discover who he is; he is an abstraction trying to become a human being; he is the son in search of a father, inhumanely rejected and abused by the inflexible father images in his life and eventually crucified in the name of the people.

Joe's grandfather is the "incredibly old and incredibly dirty" Doc Hines, an obscenely fanatical inquisitor and a peeping tom.

---

[51]   Ilse Dusoir Lind, "The Design and Meaning of *Absalom, Absalom!*", *PMLA*, LXX (December 1955), p. 887.
[52]   Malin, *William Faulkner*, p. 5.
[53]   Richard Chase, "The Stone and the Crucifixion: Faulkner's *Light in August*", *William Faulkner: Two Decades of Criticism*, ed. Frederick J. Hoffman and Olga Vickery, pp. 208-09.

At the outset of Joe's life he becomes Joe's "surrogate father".[54] Because he is a religious zealot he cannot stand the idea that Joe is the bastard son of his only daughter. Because he is an intense racist, he implants the suspicion that Joe's father is a Negro in order to give his daughter's sin a "divine purpose". Hines, therefore, conceives of the fornication of his daughter as an act of God's will.

God said to old Doc Hines. "And now I've set My will to working and now I'm gone. There aint enough sin here to keep Me busy because what do I care for the fornication of a slut, since that is a part of My purpose too.

God's purpose, as Hines sees it, is to provide the world with a physical symbol of the worst evil – miscegenation; as a part-Negro, therefore, Joe Christmas becomes "the devil's walking seed unbeknownst among them, polluting the earth with the working of that word upon him". Hines believes his divinely appointed mission is to announce God's message of judgment upon the mulatto in the person of his grandson. He heard God say, "So I am gone now, because I have set My will a-working and I can leave you here to watch it." Therefore, Hines follows Joe to the orphanage and gets a job there as janitor in order to be near the child and inform him that he is a "nigger"; as the first few years of Joe's life pass, Hines becomes sure that Joe is uncertain whether he is white or black, so he feels his work is temporarily over:

God come and He said to old Doc Hines, "You can go too now. You have done My work. There is no more evil here now but womanevil, not worthy for My chosen instrument to watch." And old Doc Hines went when God told him to go. But he kept in touch with God.[55]

As a surrogate father Hines is characterized chiefly by the attributes of a vengeful Calvinist God. He is emptied of all spontaneous love because he is obsessed with a manufactured idea of God and God's will.

As a result of his grandfather's fiendishness, Christmas begins his life in complete confusion about whether he is white or Negro.

[54]   *Ibid.*, p. 209.
[55]   *Light in August*, pp. 335-38.

When Joe is five years old and in the orphanage, Hines asks him, "Do you think you are a nigger because God has marked your face?" Joe responds by asking, "Is God a nigger too?" indicating how unsure he is just what the color differentiation means or is. Later Joe asks a Negro who works at the orphanage, "How come you are a nigger?" and then immediately adds, "I aint a nigger." The Negro responds prophetically: "You are worse than that. You don't know what you are. And more than that, you wont never know. You'll live and you'll die and you wont never know." Joe apparently feels he should make some response, so he says, "God aint no nigger"; the Negro replies, "I reckon you ought to know what God is, because dont nobody but God know what you is." Overhearing this conversation Hines is pleased there is a doubt about Joe's color because this means that he still has a mission to perform; as he says, "But God wasn't there to say, because He had set His will to working and left old Doc Hines to watch it." For twenty-eight years Hines watches for the definitive moment to fulfill his mission and judge Joe Christmas in the name of God. The moment comes when Christmas is arrested, and Hines gets the message on a divine circuit:

"That bastard, Lord! I feel! I feel the teeth and the fangs of evil!" and God said, "It's that bastard. Your work is not done yet. He's a pollution and a abomination on My earth." [56]

Doc Hines attempts to force the judgment of God by arousing a mob to lynch his grandson, an act that reveals the extent of diabolic evil in him and in the people. The grandfather will gladly condemn his grandson because Christmas is a divinely appointed sacrifice created to expose "the vengeful will of the Lord"; he must die in order to exemplify the crime and horror of miscegenation; he must die in order to save and perpetuate the social system. Hines' partially successful attempt to arouse the mob is indicative of the support his racist ideas receive from the people. His idea of Negro "contamination" excites support because it has a religious sanction through his private vision and faith. Thus this is the

[56]   *Ibid.*, pp. 335-38.

"father" that opens and closes Joe's life. His inflexibility (a pathological condition with him) is fed by the rigid dogmas of his religion and his sociology. His fatherly characteristics reflect the decayed theology of his region. As William Frohock notes, out of this theology comes "the obsessions and anxiety states of the characters which stand in the place of motives, determining their character".[57] Old grandfather Hines attempts Abraham's act, but his orders do not come from Abraham's God; his orders come from the idol of the market place.

Joe's second father is Simon McEachern, the man who takes him from the orphanage in order to make him a Presbyterian. Simon McEachern is a living symbol of the inhuman abstractness of a rigid religious doctrine; he concentrates on sin and judgment, has a fanatical devotion to religion and guides his actions by a logic that excludes any human emotion. Faulkner says that to Christmas and others he appears as "the actual representative of the wrathful and retributive Throne".[58] McEachern adopts Joe that he may "eat my bread and ... observe my religion".[59] He wishes to make Joe into a Calvinistic saint: "For I will have you learn soon that the two abominations are sloth and idle thinking, the two virtues are work and the fear of God." [60] In order to force his design upon Christmas, McEachern employs two tools – the Presbyterian catechism and a leather strap.

Faulkner shows the nature and the effects of McEachern's inflexibility in three scenes of Joe's youth. When he is eight Joe refuses to learn his catechism so McEachern beats him senseless. Joe sees that McEachern is not being unkind. He is being inhuman; that is a characteristic trait of the inflexible. "His voice was not unkind. It was not human, personal, at all. It was just cold, implacable, like written or printed words." [61] McEachern displays a satanic pride during this experience; he prays that he be forgiven for striking a child and that for Joe

[57]   William Frohock, *The Novel of Violence in America, 1920-1950* (Dallas, 1950), p. 154.
[58]   *Light in August*, p. 178.
[59]   *Ibid.*, p. 127.
[60]   *Ibid.*, p. 126.
[61]   *Ibid.*, p. 130.

. . . the sin of disobedience be forgiven him also, through the advocacy of the man whom he had flouted and disobeyed, requesting that the Almighty be as magnanimous as himself, and by and through and because of conscious grace.[62]

After the beating and McEachern's prayer Joe says, "On this day I became a man." [63] When he is fourteen Joe is still being beaten with regularity by McEachern, and he receives these punishments as though he were "a post or a tower upon which the sentient part of him mused like a hermit, contemplative and remote with ecstasy and selfcrucifixion".[64] The foster father is slowly beating his son into permanent withdrawal from man and society. At eighteen Joe sells a cow that McEachern had given him in order to get money and clothes to go into town. McEachern pursues Joe to a dance, breaking in upon him and his partner with the words, "Away Jezebel! Away harlot!" His mad pursuit of Joe and his vengeful behavior indicate that he believes he is fighting evil and the devil incarnate in the person of his son.

Perhaps they were not even his hands which struck at the face of the youth whom he had nurtured and sheltered and clothed from a child, and perhaps when the face ducked the blow and came up again it was not the face of that child. But he could not have been surprised at that, since it was not the child's face which he was concerned with: it was the face of Satan which he knew as well.

Joe is a devil because he will not fit the pattern prescribed for him by his father. Actually, of course, McEachern is not destroying Satan in the person of his son, he is destroying humanity. Faulkner suggests that when Joe smashes McEachern's head with a chair, he may have killed him; if so, this fact augments the destructive power of the father's inflexibility. Not only does the father drive the son into the treacherous arms of a whore, but he also brought death and "nothingness" upon himself. Faulkner's statement, "Perhaps the nothingness astonished him a little, but not too much, and not for long",[65] reveals the emptiness in

[62]   *Ibid.*, p. 133.
[63]   *Ibid.*, p. 128.
[64]   *Ibid.*, p. 140.
[65]   *Ibid.*, p. 178.

McEachern, his God, and his heaven. Joe's relationship with his
foster father is very neatly summarized by Mrs. Vickery who says,
"The spiritual relationship of father and son is submerged in an
intricate and deadly game of good and evil, reward and punishment." [66]

At the beginning of this discussion of *Light in August* I referred to a godfather figure who influences Joe Christmas' life.
I intended this as an ironic designation for the character Percy
Grimm. Since Grimm is the undoubted high priest of the god of
social convention in the United States of America, he is a social
representative. He is "irresistible and prophet-like" to the people
of the town, and they accept him as a representative "with respect and perhaps a little awe and a deal of actual faith and confidence".[67] An orphan is a social responsibility; society itself becomes the godparent, the one "who sponsors the newborn and
becomes responsible for its faith". Joe's refusal to accept the
"faith" of a rigid society is answered by Grimm; he becomes, as
Malin notes, "the father-image, who punishes [Joe] for his sinful
attempts at self expression".[68]

Throughout the novel, Grimm (as his name indicates) is pictured in religious terms which accentuate the inflexibility of his
nature and his role in society. In a great many ways he is like
"Hines and McEachern", says Waggoner, all of whom "in their
several ways are 'believers', but they have never repented and
their actions are unconsciously calculated to protect them from
the need to repent".[69] Faulkner refers to Grimm's god as "The
Player", an ironic term he uses when he wishes to indicate the
capriciousness of man's fate. When he is given the opportunity of
being a super-patriot, a white-racist, and an officer in the national
guard, Grimm feels the warm security of living life in a prescribed
pattern.

He could now see his life opening before him, uncomplex and inescapable as a barren corridor, completely freed now of ever again

[66] Vickery, *The Novels of William Faulkner*, p. 70.
[67] *Light in August*, pp. 397, 400.
[68] Malin, *William Faulkner*, p. 23.
[69] Waggoner, *From Jefferson to the World*, p. 106.

having to think or decide, the burden which he now assumed and carried as bright and weightless and martial as his insignatory brass.

Because he acts with the sanction of the social order and the government, he has a "blind and untroubled faith in the rightness and infallibility of his actions". The murder of a white woman by a Negro is a call to colors for Grimm. He achieves a kind of beatific splendor in his mechanized response. As he moves about organizing the search parties that will scour the town for Christmas, Faulkner says that "his face had that serene, unearthly luminousness of angels in church windows". Later, when he has Christmas trapped and is about to emasculate him, he says, " 'Jesus Christ' . . . his young voice clear and outraged like that of a young priest." [70] As a young priest, a spiritual father, Grimm performs the act of sacrifice demanded by the elect and white of the social order. But the sacrificial power entrusted to him is only a destructive urge. Under orders from his god, he does not sacrifice, he murders.

Joe Christmas is the son of these three men: Hines, McEachern, and Grimm. But of course he has no earthly father, so he is, as his name, age and position indicate, the Son of Man. Joe's position in the novel is like that position Jesus Christ holds in relation to society: he is cut off from society and yet society is forced to act in response to him, to judge him and by the judgment judge itself. Joe's suspected Negro blood is the element within him that separates him from the chosen people. Hightower asks, "Is it certain, proved, that he has Negro blood? . . . What it will mean when the people – if they catch. . . . Poor man. Poor mankind." [71] The retired minister senses that the people of the South are a dangerous group because they are rigidly structured and repressed:

Pleasure, ecstasy, they cannot seem to bear: their escape from it is in violence, in drinking and fighting and praying; catastrophe too, the violence identical and apparently unescapable. *And so why should not their religion drive them to crucifixion of themselves and one another?*

[70]   *Light in August,* pp. 395-406.
[71]   *Ibid.,* p. 87.

As he senses, they will crucify Christmas:

Gladly, gladly . . . Since to pity him would be to admit self doubt and
to hope for and need pity themselves. They will do it gladly, gladly.
That's why it is so terrible, terrible, terrible.[72]

By picturing Christmas' death as a crucifixion at the hands of the
people Faulkner intimates that contemporary religion is as rigid
as it was in Christ's day. The zealots, the religious hypocrites, and
the representatives of the chosen people will act together to ex-
terminate the Son of Man. "His blood be upon our hands" the
people cried, and Faulkner indicates that the same thing will be
true of Joe Christmas:

The pent black blood seemed to rush like a released breath. It seemed
to rush out of his pale body like the rush of sparks from a rising
rocket; upon that black blast the man seemed to rise soaring into their
memories forever and ever. They are not to lose it, in whatever peaceful valleys, beside whatever placid and reassuring streams of old age,
in the mirroring faces of whatever children they will contemplate old
disasters and newer hopes. It will be there, musing, quiet, steadfast,
not fading and not particularly threatful, but of itself alone serene, of
itself alone triumphant.[73]

Like Christ, Joe "ascends" and lives "forever and ever", a clear
indication that the "serene and triumphant" quality in the Son of
Man will prevail over the inflexibility and destructive force of the
"fathers" of mankind who prefer Barrabas to Christ.

In *Escape from Freedom*, Erich Fromm offers a good analysis
of the man who is really trying to flee from the complex problem
of evaluation and decision that being free entails. The rigid character is the one who has exchanged the awful burden of being free
for the miracle, mystery, and authority of the Grand Inquisitor of
Dostoevski. Fromm feels that such a man is subject to compulsive
patterning and shows a tendency toward escape, "in the process
of which the isolated individual becomes an automaton, loses his
self, and yet at the same time consciously conceives of himself as
free and subject only to himself".[74] The fathers in Faulkner's

---

[72]   *Ibid.*, p. 322.
[73]   *Ibid.*, p. 407.
[74]   Erich Fromm, *Escape from Freedom* (New York, 1951), p. 241.

tragic novels are characterized in just this way. Their loss of freedom is a loss of motion and response, revealing an absence of
psychological strength; consequently, they need a design to speak
for them and give them security. Inflexibility is the symptom of a
loss of freedom. Inflexible man can learn nothing new, must live
by the past, and by dogma. He resists with violence the threat of
change. Furthermore, violence is a clue to the unreasonableness
of the individual and the pattern. The lack of psychological
strength, the loss of freedom, and the recourse to violence are
qualities which characterize a man who cannot stand alone. Per
sonality within the design is inhuman because it cannot take the
risk of being in motion, of being alive.

Faulkner regards the ideal man as one who can adapt to change
while in "the furious motion of being alive".[75] Man in motion is
man responsive; as one of his heroes, Gavin Stevens, puts it, "I
also am Motion",[76] meaning that in the flux of time he is capable
of entertaining new truth and modifying the pattern of his life
and culture. By showing it is the father who lacks motion, Faulkner shows the critical effect of unresponsiveness in a family
situation. The father cannot respond or answer to the human
situation – symbolized by the son – and his effect therefore is
destructive. The son's search for the father is the search for love,
for a worthy guide, for an authority that is dependable. Malin
feels that this pattern of search is used so repeatedly by Faulkner
"it assumes a crucial place in his myth"; he explains the myth in
this way:

Faulkner believed that he could concrete his themes of the rigidity of
personal compulsion and social organization through the use of the
father image. He believed he could symbolize the rebellion against
environmental evils, the quest for new values, through his use of the
son ... The son recognizes the fact that his father refuses to consider
his personal doubts. The father is too intent upon his own compulsive
behavior to take time to look at any problems which, he believes, do
not pertain to his own design.[77]

Indeed, it does seem that Faulkner's repeated use of the father-

---

[75] Gwynn and Blotner, *Faulkner in the University*, p. 239.
[76] *The Town*, p. 135.
[77] Malin, *William Faulkner*, p. 16.

son situation is what Richard Chase would call a quest for myth. The constant repetition of this pattern in the tragic fiction leaves no doubt that one of the primary forces of destruction in Faulkner's tragic world is a rooted, impassive, motionless father, projecting his personal compulsions through a tightly patterned way of life.

II. THE WILDERNESS AND THE SPIRITUAL FATHER

> The wilderness the old bear ran was his college
> and the old male bear itself, so long unwifed
> and childless as to have become its own un-
> gendered progenitor, was his alma mater.[1]

"The Bear" is a pivotal artistic creation in Faulkner's career. In it he expresses all of the creative themes that are developed in four subsequent works: *Intruder in the Dust, Requiem for a Nun, A Fable* and *Snopes*. The story was actually written in sections before it was combined and revised to become a portion of the novel *Go Down Moses*. Faulkner first published a story called "Lion" in *Harpers Magazine,* December, 1935; then, on May 9, 1942, he published "The Bear" in *Saturday Evening Post*. By combining the two stories with other material, he got the effect he wanted for the version that appeared in the novel *Go Down Moses*. The essence of what he wished to express is fivefold: (1) the possibility of gaining love and learning through the mediation of a surrogate parent, (2) the confrontation of spiritual life through the wilderness, (3) the bond of humanity that unites mankind, (4) the necessity of repudiating evil and (5) the creative power of a life lived in worthiness, humility and courage. These five purposes express for Faulkner the full meaning of being creatively and furiously alive, which he metaphorically pictures as being in motion. The expression of these creative themes, following as it does his great period of tragic fiction, has been called by R. W. B. Lewis "a robust and formidable act of artistic

---

[1] *Go Down Moses*, p. 210.

conversion".[2] As Lewis suggests, however, there is some question whether his liberation is helpful to his career as a novelist, for the fiction that embodies his creative themes also displays a distinct loss of dramatic power as well.

As surprising as it may seem, there is a persistent refusal on the part of critical writers to consider "The Bear" an integral part of *Go Down Moses*. I cannot account for this critical tendency; all I can say is that it presents an impoverished view of the story. *Go Down Moses* is structured around two themes: white injustice to the Negro in the person of Lucas Beauchamp, a character more fully developed in *Intruder in the Dust*, and the nobility of character learned from the wilderness by Ike Mc-Caslin. There is no doubt, of course, that McCaslin's story is the central part of the book, dominating as it does the sections entitled "Was", "The Old People", "The Bear", and "Delta Autumn". But while the stories of Lucas and Ike run along separately in the novel, the themes are united when Isaac discovers that his grandfather committed Sutpen's sin in refusing to say, "My son" to a Negro.[3] Thus the novel introduces again the evil of an inhumane father who wants to perpetuate an established way of life and a son who finds he must define the nature of his own existence in relation to this discovered evil. "The Bear" section of the novel can be interpreted as a contemporary expression of a favorite American theme: the discovery of evil by an innocent boy who is coming to maturity in a complex world. Cooper and Twain, in their way and for their time, examined the same problem; there are many parallels between Natty Bumppo, Huck Finn, and Ike McCaslin. The frontier, the river and the wilderness stand for the uncorrupted Garden of Eden; civilization is the evil, and the experience of the hero is the reaction of uncorrupted conscience. These materials constitute what R. W. B. Lewis in *The American Adam* refers to as "the matter of Adam", the myth of the American encounter with history and innocence.[4] The symbolism involved in this myth is,

[2]   R. W. B. Lewis, *The Picaresque Saint* (New York, 1959), p. 180.
[3]   *Go Down Moses*, p. 269.
[4]   R. W. B. Lewis, *The Amercian Adam* (Chicago, 1955), p. 127.

according to Feidelson, merely a way of getting at real subject matter.[5] I think, therefore, we must examine *Go Down Moses* as the conceptual antithesis of inflexibility expressed in figurative terms.

The history of Ike McCaslin begins in "The Old People" section of *Go Down Moses*. The old people are Sam Fathers, part Negro and part Indian, and Jobaker, a full-blooded Chickasaw; they possess the love and wisdom of nature and life that gives them a paternal position with Ike. Ike is orphaned as a young boy, and Sam Fathers (as his name suggests) becomes his spiritual father. "He taught the boy the woods, to hunt, when to shoot and when not to shoot, when to kill and when not to kill, and better, what to do with it afterward. Then he would talk to the boy." [6] When Ike is initiated into manhood through a ritualistic slaying of an animal, Sam Fathers is standing just behind him as he had been standing when the boy shot his first running rabbit.[7] After Ike kills the buck Sam wipes the blood across his face baptizing him into the life and death cycle in nature. All along Sam has assured him, "You wait. You'll be a hunter. You'll be a man." [8] Through his instruction and his faith in him, Ike feels that Sam has "already consecrated and absolved him from weakness and regret".[9] And time and again through his life Ike remembers this and says, "Sam Fathers set me free." [10] When Ike is nine, Sam announces that he wishes to leave the plantation and go live alone in the wilderness. "What about Isaac here", Sam is asked, "how will you get away from him?" [11] But Ike knows Sam can leave, for together they have had a revelation in the wilderness insuring Ike's spiritual maturity. On a great hunt together, Ike and Sam have heard the leader of the party kill a great buck. When Ike hears the hunting horn blow, he starts to make for the

---

[5] Charles Feidelson, Jr., *Symbolism and American Literature* (Chicago, 1953), p. 5.
[6] *Go Down Moses*, p. 170.
[7] *Ibid.*, p. 163.
[8] *Ibid.*, p. 176.
[9] *Ibid.*, p. 182.
[10] *Ibid.*, p. 300.
[11] *Ibid.*, p. 173.

kill, but Sam says, "Wait." "What for?" responds Ike; "Don't you hear that horn?"

And he would remember how Sam was standing. Sam had not moved ... Sam did not even see him. Then the boy saw the buck ... Then it saw them. And still it did not begin to run. It just stopped for an instant, taller than any man, looking at them; then its muscles suppled, gathered. It did not even alter its course, not fleeing, not even running, just moving with that winged and effortless ease ... passing within twenty feet of them, its head high and the eye not proud and not haughty but just full and wild and unafraid, and Sam standing beside the boy now, his right arm raised at full length, palm-outward, speaking in that tongue which the boy had learned from listening to him and Joe Baker in the blacksmith shop, while up on the ridge Walter Ewell's horn was still blowing them in to a dead buck.

"Oleh, Chief", Sam said. "Grandfather".[12]

In the shade of the slain deer Sam has shown Ike "the father of Spirits", the grandfather of all deer. Later when Ike tells his cousin of the experience, he is incredulous, saying "Suppose they don't have a substance, can't cast a shadow", to which Ike cries out, "But I saw it ... I saw him!" [13] Through the mediation of his spiritual father, the boy has seen the great father of life; in addition his father has taught him well and baptized him into a worthy life where violence has meaning. Ike is thus prepared for confirmation. Having been prepared by the old people, he is now ready to face the wilderness and the old bear.

Ike passes through a series of experiences with the wilderness and the old bear that make his education complete. As Faulkner says, "If Sam Fathers had been his mentor and the backyard rabbits and squirrels his kindergarten, then the wilderness the old bear ran was his college and the old male bear itself, so long un-wifed and childless as to have become its own ungendered pro-genitor, was his alma mater." [14] Faulkner also suggests through religious metaphors that Ike's is a spiritual education as well. For instance, Faulkner notes that Ike enters into "his novitiate to the true wilderness with Sam beside him" as his spiritual guardian;

12   *Ibid.*, pp. 183-84.
13   *Ibid.*, p. 187.
14   *Ibid.*, p. 210.

the Fall hunt is the "yearly pageant-rite of the old bear's furious immortality". Thus Ike begins to realize (because he has been prepared) that "at the age of ten he was witnessing his own birth".[15] Ike is coming to man's estate, and the last thing he must learn in order to be completely free lies hidden in the wilderness, and the old bear himself must become the final teacher.

The wilderness that Ike seeks to know and understand is symbolized by the bear. The fact that no hunter can ever kill the bear or see anything of it, except its huge tracks, represents the enduring and immortal seed of life that lies hidden in the primitive woods. A fear of this life is reflected in the unworthy men, the unlearned, unskilled and irreverent land-seekers, who attempt to trap or slaughter the bear. These men regard the wilderness as an enemy.

It was as if the boy had already divined what his senses and intellect had not encompassed yet: that doomed wilderness whose edges were being constantly and punily gnawed at by men with plows and axes who feared it because it was wilderness, men myriad and nameless even to one another in the land where the old bear had earned a name, and through which ran not even a mortal beast but an anachronism indomitable and invincible out of an old dead time, a phantom, epitome and apotheosis of the old wild life . . . the old bear, solitary, indomitable and alone; widowered childless and absolved of mortality.[16]

In contrast to the greedy speculators who know nothing of the mysteries of the wilderness, there are the old people, like Sam and the Negroes who "knew things that had been tamed out of our blood so long ago that we have not only forgotten them, we have to live together in herds to protect ourselves from our own sources".[17] Ike's hunting party seeks to establish contact with the primary source of man's life and sustenance through the ritualistic pursuit of the bear; as Faulkner points out, "they were going not to hunt bear and deer but to keep yearly rendezvous with the bear which they did not even intend to kill".[18]

In his eleventh year Ike learns what it means to completely

15   *Ibid.*, pp. 194-95.
16   *Ibid.*, pp. 193-94.
17   *Ibid.*, p. 167.
18   *Ibid.*, p. 194.

relinquish himself in full trust to the wilderness. As he is out on his own tracking the bear through the wilderness, he senses the presence of the great animal all about him, but he is vouchsafed no vision. Back at camp, Sam tells him "It's the gun. . . . You will have to choose", Sam says. Ike follows Sam's instructions and leaves the gun. When he puts out into the wilderness again, he still does not see the bear. He realizes that leaving the gun is not enough, and senses that his watch and compass are an impediment because they represent the taint of time and space – civilization. He must bring only himself in trust to the wilderness. This time as he enters the wilderness he gets lost. Three times he seeks to discover his own tracks always doing what Sam had coached and drilled him to do. Still he is lost. Suddenly he spots tracks that are not his own; they belong to the bear, and they keep appearing before him mysteriously. The tracks lead him back to the little glade where he started, and he sees the watch and compass gleaming on the bush where he left them. "Then he saw the bear. It did not emerge, appear; it was just there . . . then it faded, sank back into the wilderness without motion." [19] Because he "relinquished completely" to the wilderness, Ike, who was lost, is saved and has a vision of primitive life itself – a look at the old bear.

The second time Ike sees the bear he learns something of courage. Ike and Sam slip off to the wilderness to test a little mongrel dog, "of the sort called fyce by the negroes, a ratter, itself not much bigger than a rat and possessing that sort of courage which had long since stopped being bravery and had become foolhardiness". When the fyce attacks the bear that they have ambushed, Ike runs out to save the dog.

When he overtook and grasped the shrill, frantically pinwheeling little dog, it seemed to him that he was directly under the bear. He could smell it, strong and hot and rank. Sprawling, he looked up where it loomed and towered over him like a thunderclap. It was quite familiar, until he remembered: this was the way he had used to dream about it.
Then it was gone.

Despite the fact that he could have killed the bear ("You've

[19]   *Ibid.*, pp. 206-09.

done seed him twice now . . . This time you couldn't have missed him", says Sam) and the bear could have killed him, both have refrained from an unmeaningful slaughter in the face of courage. The little fyce had shown the kind of bravery a dog must possess to hunt the bear. Sam says "You's almost the one we wants . . . You just ain't big enough. We aint got that one yet . . . Somebody is going to someday." Sam knows that a proper dog will be found and that Ben must be killed because his home, the wilderness, is being eaten up by the lumber companies. Ike is also aware that the old bear must be hunted and killed, and he knows one of the initiated must do it and that the bear will permit it. "I know it", the boy said. "That's why it must be one of us. So it wont be until the last day. When even he dont want it to last any longer." [20]

In time a fit dog is found and named Lion, and the great hunt follows, bringing the resolution of Ike's experience with the bear. Ike and Sam know what the death of the old bear means: the total disappearance of the wilderness. Yet both see it is inevitable. As Ike reflects:

So he should have hated and feared Lion. Yet he did not. It seemed to him there was a fatality in it. It seemed to him that something, he didn't know what, was beginning; had already begun. It was like the last act on a set stage. It was the beginning of the end of something, he didn't know what except that he would not grieve. He would be humble and proud that he had been found worthy to be a part of it. [21]

When the old bear is tracked down by Lion and killed in hand-to-hand combat by Boon Hogganbeck, the end of an era is heralded. The wilderness and life as Sam Fathers knew it is now gone, and Sam gives up the will to live, preferring to join Old Ben and Lion in the earth, "and only the boy knew that Sam too was going to die". [22] Sam gets Boon to kill him and bury him Indian style on a platform. With the death of his spiritual father, and the destruction of the totem in Old Ben, Ike is ready now to assume the full responsibilities for his own life and the land he will inherit when

[20] *Ibid.*, pp. 211-12.
[21] *Ibid.*, p. 226.
[22] *Ibid.*, p. 246.

he is twenty-one. The beginning and end that he has seen is, as
Lewis observes,

A vast drama of death and birth: the death of Old Ben, of Sam
Fathers (Ike's foster-parent and tutor), of the dog Lion, of the wilderness and the companionship Ike had known there, of an entire world.[23]

Ike becomes the atavism of the wilderness values: freedom, courage, pride, humility, and the will to endure.

In the same year of the great hunt, Ike has another important
experience. Now in his sixteenth year, he begins an examination
of the plantation record books. By piecing together many entries,
with some decidedly clever deductions, he discovers that his
grandfather, Carrothers McCaslin, had bought a colored slave,
Eunice, and, when she was pregnant by him, married her off to
another slave, Thucydis. Twenty-three years after, Eunice drown-
ed herself because she discovered that Carrothers McCaslin had
made their daughter pregnant. Ike realizes with a shock that his
inheritance in the land should be shared with his colored cousins,
the offspring of Eunice's children. The refusal of his grandfather
to recognize his part-colored grandson seems a terrible wrong to
Ike. When he discovers that his grandfather had arranged for the
children to get one thousand dollars upon coming of age, Ike
thinks, "*So I reckon that was cheaper than saying My son to a
nigger . . . Even if My son wasn't but just two words. But there
must have been love . . . Some sort of love. Even what he would
have called love: not just an afternoon's or a night's spittoon.*" [24]
But he discovers no love; he only discovers that his grandfather
abused the Negroes, refused to recognize his son, committed incest with his daughter, and tried to atone for the whole affair
with money because he regarded these people as mere entries in a
ledger. To Ike, however, the ledger is the revelation of a "general
and condoned injustice [with] its slow amortization [and] the specific tragedy which had not been condoned and could never be
amortized".[25] His grandfather's action epitomizes the evil of
Southern history, and when Ike is twenty-one years old, he re-

[23]   Lewis, *The Picaresque Saint*, p. 201.
[24]   *Go Down Moses*, pp. 269-70.
[25]   *Ibid.*, p. 266.

pudiates his inheritance because of the evil he has discovered and feels he must stand against. Since Ike makes his discovery in the plantation commissary, that is where he makes his repudiation: "not against the wilderness but against the land, not in pursuit and lust but in relinquishment, and in the commissary as it should have been, not the heart perhaps but certainly the solar-plexus of the repudiated and relinquished".[26] Ike relinquishes his right to the land and repudiates the evil done by his family in order to break the curse that hangs over him and the land. "Don't you see?" he cries. "Don't you see? This whole land, the whole South, is cursed, and all of us who derive from it, whom it ever suckled, white and black both, lie under the curse." [27] Waggoner expertly summarizes the meaning of this portion of the novel:

Part IV of "The Bear" gives us Isaac's discovery of the evil that made the purification rite necessary, makes explicit the content of the wisdom learned from the wilderness, and shows us something of the result of the boy's attempting to live what he has learned.[28]

The next section of "The Bear" relates how Ike engages his cousin, Cass Edmonds, in a long discourse in which he develops the idea that the evil within the South and man is really a revelation of the destructive nature of a "design" and "original sin". One of the first things Ike tells Cass is that God created the earth and gave man dominion over it, "and all the fee He asked was pity and humility and sufferance and endurance".[29] Time and again, however, man proved unworthy; time and again man was "dispossessed of Eden", until God "used a simple egg to discover to them a new world where a nation of people could be founded in humility and pity and sufferance and pride of one to another".[30] The new world is America, a new Eden, and Ike is examining the whole history of the race and man to find out what went wrong. Ike comes to see the new world was never devoid of evil, that it was "already tainted even before any white man

[26]   *Ibid.*, p. 255.
[27]   *Ibid.*, p. 278.
[28]   Waggoner, *From Jefferson to the World*, p. 206.
[29]   *Go Down Moses*, p. 257.
[30]   *Ibid.*, p. 258.

owned it by what Grandfather and his kind, his fathers, had brought into the new land . . . as though in the sailfuls of the old world's tainted wind which drove the ships".[31] The taint of Ike's fathers, as Lewis notes, "is the evil of slavery, rooted in the sin of spiritual pride and the lust of possession", which they seek to protect through an inflexible projection of a highly structured way of life. Furthermore, Ike sees that what Grandfather and his kind brought with them into the New World was themselves; Lewis explains, "what they brought was the nature of man".[32] And Ike's attempt to repudiate the design and original sin comes as a result of his freedom – from fear, lust, greed, intolerance, pride – which he learned from a father who originally liberated him: "Yes", says Ike, "Sam Fathers set me free." [33]

Ike's somewhat qualified stand for positive moral values comes slowly and only after he has probed the inhumanity of his ancestor's way of life. When he is eighteen, Ike makes a pilgrimage back to the wilderness to visit the graves of Old Ben, Lion, and Sam Fathers. Now the railroad has obliterated the trails, and the logging company is chewing the wilderness to bits. But Ike still has the vision: "The wilderness soared, musing, inattentive, myriad, eternal, green; older than any mill-shed, longer than any spur-line." [34] When he arrives at the site of the graves, he experiences another epiphany: there is no death in the wilderness. "That place where dissolution itself was a seething turmoil of ejaculation tumescence conception and birth, and death did not even exist." [35] His vision is repeated and enlarged; he sees:

There was no death, not Lion and not Sam: not held fast in earth but free in earth and not in earth but of earth, myriad yet undiffused of every myriad part, leaf and twig and particle, air and sun and rain and dew and night, acorn oak and leaf and acorn again, dark and dawn and dark and dawn again in their immutable progression and, being myriad, one: and old Ben too, Old Ben too.[36]

[31]   *Ibid.*, p. 259.
[32]   Lewis, *The Picaresque Saint*, p. 206.
[33]   *Go Down Moses*, p. 300.
[34]   *Ibid.*, p. 322.
[35]   *Ibid.*, p. 327.
[36]   *Ibid.*, pp. 328-29.

Ike now sees life as but stages in a unified order; he sees a oneness implicit in the cyclic progression of all life forms; life is ceaseless motion. It is also on this same pilgrimage, three years prior to his repudiation of evil, that Ike acknowledges the true parents that have enabled him to become a flexible, responsive, free man, capable of learning and change:

... summer, and fall, and snow, and wet and saprife spring in their ordered immortal sequence, the deathless and immemorial phases of the mother who had shaped him if any had toward the man he almost was, mother and father both to the old man born of a Negro slave and a Chickasaw chief who had been his spirit's father if any had.[37]

Later, when he is twenty-one, Ike comes to feel himself a part of the family of man too, for the evil of private ownership and slavery must be succeeded by "the communal anonymity of brotherhood", created by God so that man can hold "the earth mutual and intact" apart from a rigid and inhuman design. All that God asks of man is "pity and humility and sufferance and endurance, and the sweat of his face for bread".[38] So as a final and total gesture of repudiation and atonement Ike becomes a carpenter thinking "if the Nazarene had found carpentering good for the life and ends He had assumed and elected to serve, it would be all right too for Isaac McCaslin".[39] The intent and meaning of Ike's stand for moral values is well stated by Lewis who calls him a "picaresque saint":

... humanity can be asserted only in a refusal to be contaminated by the humanity of others; that in order to become a man, one must leap beyond the condition and company of men, and take upon one's self the role of the solitary and purely saintly redeemer.[40]

Speaking of another hero of the wilderness, Natty Bumppo, D. H. Lawrence concludes his essay with these observations about "the essential American": "A man who keeps his moral integrity hard and intact. An isolate, almost selfless, stoic, enduring man,

---

[37] *Ibid.*, p. 326.
[38] *Ibid.*, p. 257.
[39] *Ibid.*, p. 309.
[40] Lewis, *The Picaresque Saint*, p. 219.

who lives by death, by killing, but who is pure white." [41] These words fit Ike McCaslin as well as Natty Bumppo, and I believe that both Cooper and Faulkner intend to show how a hero, properly initiated, may behave in the presence of evil. The evil dominant in Faulkner's tragic novels is seen in a different perspective through the character of Isaac McCaslin. As Lewis observes,

Beginning with "The Bear", and there more emphatically than anywhere else, what is positive in human nature and the moral world envelops and surrounds what is evil. The corrupting and the destructive and the desperate have their ageless being in human experience, but here they become known to us exactly in their opposition, even their subordination, to the creative and nourishing.[42]

Thus Ike McCaslin becomes a man through the creative and nourishing force of the wilderness, undoes evil, and emerges as Lawrence's "selfless, stoic, enduring man".

However, in order to judge accurately of the wilderness as a creative force it would be well to consider it apart from the character of Ike McCaslin. The wilderness is to Faulkner what it has been to a host of American idealists, including Emerson, Thoreau and Whitman – a source of truth and beauty. Faulkner once said, "The beauty, spiritual and physical, of the South lies in the fact that God has done so much for it and man so little." [43] As he writes of this beauty, Faulkner's prose achieves an almost hallucinatory power when he seeks to represent the ethereal and the mystical. He measures man's acts against truth and beauty, using nature as a norm. Campbell and Foster say that

. . . in the fictional world which he creates, Faulkner often sets up his view of nature as a norm on which he constructs his story. For him nature suggests at least these attributes as a norm for human conduct: endurance, honesty, courage, physical contact with nature and tolerant pessimism.[44]

[41] D. H. Lawrence, *Studies in Classic American Literature* (New York, 1953), p. 73.
[42] Lewis, *The Picaresque Saint*, p. 194.
[43] *Salamagundi*, p. 37.
[44] Harry Modean Campbell and Ruel E. Foster, *William Faulkner* (Norman, Okla., 1951), p. 146.

Faulkner believes that in nature man can learn the truths of the human heart; as he has put it, "There may be something he could substitute for the ruined wilderness, but he hasn't found that." [45] Nature as a definer of truth is well illustrated in "The Bear". Ike is told by his uncle that his refusal to kill the bear when he had the opportunity is a courageous affirmation of life and a key to truth. Quoting Keats, the uncle says, "She cannot fade, though thou hast not thy bliss, . . . Forever wilt thou love and she be fair." He explains to Ike that Keats "was talking about truth. Truth is one. It covers all things which touch the heart." And Ike comes to see that in his refusal to slay, he has acted from the heart and thus gained truth: "Courage and honor and pride, and pity and love of justice and of liberty. They all touch the heart, and what the heart holds to becomes truth, as far as we know truth." [46] Thus Faulkner sees the wilderness as more than a mystic life source; the correct response to the life source leads man to the things that touch his heart, and these become for him truth. It is the wilderness which puts man in motion enabling him to arrive at these discoveries.

It is very difficult not to respect and respond to Faulkner's view of the wilderness, yet it is equally difficult to fully accept it. His views as presented in *Go Down Moses* are one-sided: the wilderness or nothing. But judging from his remarks at the University of Virginia in 1958, he now recognizes that the population explosion demands the wilderness give way for living space. Faulkner expressed his more balanced view in these words:

If the reason for the change is base in motive – that is, to clear the wilderness, just to make cotton land, to raise cotton on an agrarian economy of peonage, slavery, it's base because it's not as good as the wilderness which it replaces. But if in the end that makes more education for more people, and more food for more people, more of the good things in life . . . then it was worth destroying the wilderness. But if all the destruction of the wilderness does is to give more people more automobiles just to ride around in, then the wilderness was better.[47]

[45]   Gwynn and Blotner, *Faulkner in the University*, p. 68.
[46]   *Go Down Moses*, p. 297.
[47]   Gwynn and Blotner, *Faulkner in the University*, p. 277.

I believe the word that expresses Faulkner's view of an ideal rela-uonship to the wilderness is "stewardship". Waggoner, who first used the word in this context, believes that Faulkner feels "Whatever destroys community and stewardship over nature . . . is evil; but the use of nature itself is not evil." [48] This observation is helpful, but it is always fairly easy to identify evil in Faulkner; what we need now to see is how the wilderness becomes a creative force, a good, instead of a vague philosophical statement of good. Perhaps something like this cannot be demonstrated, but we do know the specific evil represented by an inflexible father; we do see with precision how this evil enters the life of a son, and we can see the son's actions in terms of the evil. But Ike's interaction with the good (in Sam and in the wilderness) is never dramatized but just related, as is Ike's discovery of family evil. Essentially "The Bear" section of *Go Down Moses* lacks dramatic power; this causes Faulkner's view of the wilderness as creative force – the mythic life source, the supreme example of truth-beauty, the sponsor of moral truth in man – to be a less satisfying fictional achievement and a less believable human experience.

I believe the character of Isaac McCaslin demonstrates the in-completeness of Faulkner's concept of the wilderness. He is not a fully satisfying redeemer, for he only repudiates evil; he never acts against it. This is not enough even for Faulkner: "Well, I think a man ought to do more than just repudiate. He should have been more affirmative than just shunning people." [49] On the posi-tive side, Ike has learned some practical virtues (courage, justice, pride, humility, love); he has joined the human race, and he has repudiated the sins of the fathers. But, on the negative side, he has taken no action to correct the abuses; in a way he selfishly seeks a monastic life to escape from the public expressions of courage and love demanded of a true redeemer, a man in motion. In the words of an old hymn, "he breaks the power of cancelled sin; he sets the prisoner free", but that's all. Ike is free, but not engaged. He is not, as R. W. B. Lewis believes, the hero in the

---

[48]   Waggoner, *From Jefferson to the World*, p. 208.
[49]   Cynthia Grenier, "The Art of Fiction: An Interview with William Faulkner – September, 1955", *Accent*, Summer 1956, p. 175.

new world because his action remains self-centered. As Hoffman points out, "his quixotic gesture leads to no genuinely worthwhile results. Ike's decision, far from being a positive 'penance' for the sins of his fathers, is in the end a demonstration of weakness." [50]

The best example of Ike's incompleteness as a hero is shown in "Delta Autumn". The problem facing Ike in "Delta Autumn" is, once again, miscegenation. Ike has been explaining that the right attitude toward nature leads to the right attitude toward man. But when a Negress comes with her child, the son of Roth Edmonds, to claim a husband and father, Ike puts her off and thinks, "*Maybe in a thousand or two thousand years in America. . . . But not now! Not now!*" [51] Then he gives the infant son a hunting horn that belonged to General Compson and sends the Negress away. Roth Edmonds has sinned, to be sure, but Ike McCaslin has demonstrated a little inflexibility of his own in a father-son situation. O'Connor gives a good final assessment of Ike and his position in the entire novel. "The theme of the wisdom to be derived from the wilderness, even in its great prophet Ike, is merely juxtaposed against the theme of the injustice to the Negro. His silent exclamation merely acknowledges, it does not materially modify the injustice." [52] Faulkner himself regards Ike as unable to solve some problems. He recently said:

Well there are some people in any time and age that cannot face and cope with the problems. There seem to be three stages: The first says, This is rotten, I'll have no part of it, I will take death first, the second says, This is rotten, I don't like it, I can't do anything about it, but at least I will not participate in it myself, I will go off into a cave or climb a pillar to sit on. The third says, This stinks and I'm going to do something about it. McCaslin is the second. He says, This is bad, and I will withdraw from it. What we need are people who will say, This is bad and I'm going to do something about it. I'm going to change it.[53]

Despite the vague rendition of the wilderness and the incomplete

50   Hoffman, *William Faulkner*, p. 98.
51   *Go Down Moses*, p. 361.
52   O'Connor, *The Tangled Fire of William Faulkner*, p. 134.
53   Gwynn and Blotner, *Faulkner in the University*, pp. 245-46.

heroism of Ike McCaslin, the fact remains that nature as teacher and norm is the primary creative force in all of Faulkner's fiction informing and measuring all other creative forces and virtues: mother-love, civic morality, and brotherly love. O'Connor's final judgment of the wilderness theme is much too severe:

The treatment of the spirit of the wilderness has no real relevance beyond acknowledging a former and continuing wrong. It relates to a world not merely prior to slavery, but prior to civilization. It is kind of a neurotic dream, an escape from rather than an attempt to solve the present injustice.[54]

O'Connor fails to consider all of the psychological implications in the wilderness theme. Faulkner is primarily concerned with the Jungian process of "individuation", an experience involving the individual's clear analysis and reaction to the past and the present in relation to himself. Ike may be a half-way hero, but he is at least half-way. The unnamed corporal in *A Fable* may be his successor, but Ike is a prototype. Ike's process of becoming an individual involves what Jung calls "the myth of the hero".

The myth of the hero is the myth of our own suffering unconscious, which has an unquenchable longing for all the deepest sources of our own being; for the body of the mother, and through it for her communion with infinite life in the countless forms of existence.[55]

Ike may be interpreted, therefore, as modern man in search of a soul, and the trials he endures may be seen as the sloughing off of restrictive designs that refuse to let him be someone. In this light we may view the hunt symbolically. Malin points out that "the hunt in Faulkner's novels is the ritualistic preparation for an understanding of individual standards of behavior which reject the rigidity of the personal design".[56] And Faulkner says that to him, "The hunt [is] simply a symbol of pursuit. Most of anyone's life is a pursuit of something. That is, the only alternative to life is immobility, which is death." [57] What Ike is "hunting" for and

[54] O'Connor, *The Tangled Fire of William Faulkner*, p. 134.
[55] Carl Jung, *Psychology of the Unconscious*, trans. Beatrice M. Hinkle (New York, 1943), p. 231.
[56] Malin, *William Faulkner*, p. 85.
[57] Gwynn and Blotner, *Faulkner in the University*, p. 271.

what he finds that Faulkner's other sick, young, troubled sons do not find, is a worthy means of "pursuing" a life goal, a goal free of a design pressed by an inflexible anti-life figure. I think Faulkner's own words make this very clear:

The protagonist could have been anything else besides that bear. I simply told a story which was a natural, normal part of anyone's life in familiar and to me interesting terms without any intent to put symbolism in it. I was simply telling something which was in this case the child – the need, the compulsion of the child to adjust to the adult world. It's how he does it, how he survives it, *whether he is destroyed by trying to adjust to the adult world* or whether despite his small size he does adjust within his capacity. And always to learn something, to learn something of – not only to pursue but to overtake *and then to have the compassion not to destroy,* to catch, to touch, and then let go because then tomorrow you can pursue again. If you destroy it, what you caught, then it's gone, it's finished. And that to me is sometimes the greater part of valor but always it's the greater part of pleasure, not to destroy what *you have pursued.* The pursuit is the thing, not the reward, not the gain.[58]

In a word, the wilderness is a positive creative force because it calls for the hunt, a ritualistic pattern of human behavior in which the individual may learn how to worthily pursue a goal (being in motion, being alive) apart from the necessity to destroy in order to preserve.

For all their shortcomings in presentation and development, the wilderness and Ike McCaslin demonstrate the alternating tension that operates in the body of Faulkner's fiction. This tension, the possibility of good, is explored and defined by a modern Adam who engages in an age-old ritual to see if a good life can be lived in an evil world. He is willing, like Huck Finn, to go to civilization's hell if necessary, and he will dispossess himself of Eden in order to confess the curse. Even if he does not combat the workings of the curse in his world, he knows the curse is there. Although he is passive in the struggle to reclaim Eden, he knows the job is to be done.

[58] *Ibid.,* pp. 271-72. Italics mine.

WOMAN

III. FEMALE LUST

> Then suddenly Wilbourne heard his own voice speaking
> out of an amazed and quiet incredulity; it seemed to him
> that they both stood now, aligned, embattled and doomed
> and lost, before the entire female principle.
>
> *The Wild Palms*[1]

In *Heiress of All the Ages* William Wasserstrom discusses sex
and sentiment in the genteel tradition. He feels the American
dream of a unified society living in freedom came to be symbolized in "The American Girl", and he indicates that he received
this idea from Henry James. He goes on to say:

If this society is the heir of all the ages, she is the heiress. It became
therefore her duty to resolve and transcend all antitheses. When she
failed, the result in literature was tragic. But when she brought off
the victory, she paid the nation's debt to history and thereby perform-
ed the solemn, heroic office of the heiress of all the ages.[2]

Faulkner's women are, of course, a long way from the genteel
tradition; in fact, he invariably uses women to display the destructive power of sexual irresponsibility. As a result, the women he
creates are not mere anti-virgins; they are, as Leslie Fiedler says,
women of power and evil.

[Faulkner] reminds us (again and again!) that men are helpless in the
hands of their mothers, wives, and sisters; that females do not think
but proceed from evidence to conclusions by paths too devious for
males to follow; that they possess neither morality nor honor; that

---

[1] *The Wild Palms*, p. 57.
[2] William Wasserstrom, *Heiress of All the Ages* (Minneapolis, 1959),
p. x.

they are capable, therefore, of betrayal without qualm or quiver of guilt . . . that they are unforgiving and without charity to members of their own sex . . . that they use their sexuality with cold calculation to achieve their inscrutable ends.[3]

Faulkner's tragic fiction typically features women who do not have a moral vision capable of unifying their desires for sex, love and freedom. When a woman will not or cannot unify the desire for sex, love and freedom, she becomes malignant.

When a woman is right and good, by Faulkner's standards, she loves; she loves her man and her children. When she is wrong and evil, she uses her freedom to gain sex instead of love and is irresponsible toward her man and her children. In his early fiction there are few good women. With the exception of Dilsey, the women who figure prominently in the action are evil. As he sees it, the typical woman produced by modern society is selfish and carnal; consequently, his women reflect the moral vacuum in society itself.

Through numerous direct assertions in a variety of novels, Faulkner associates the female with evil. Maxwell Geismar observes this association and he believes that Faulkner is distressed with modern life and uses the female to exhibit the evil in the age. But Geismar is wrong when he intimates that Faulkner hates women (he calls it "The Great Hatred") and the Negro as well, that these are his twin Furies which he uses to express a larger hatred of his age.[4] Faulkner doesn't hate either the female or the Negro (consider only Dilsey whom Mr. Geismar never mentions), but he does use lovelessness and irresponsibility in women as signs of their inherent evil. Time and again, as Mr. Fiedler says, Faulkner states that women are evil, but he never says he hates them. Faulkner's typical expression is voiced by Mr. Compson who says, "Women do have . . . an affinity for evil, for believing that no woman is to be trusted, but that some men are too innocent to protect themselves." [5] On another occasion he says:

---

[3] Leslie Fiedler, *Love and Death in the American Novel* (New York, 1960), p. 309.
[4] Maxwell Geismar, *Writers in Crisis* (New York, 1947), pp. 141-84.
[5] *The Sound and the Fury*, p. 124.

Women are like that they don't acquire knowledge ... they have an affinity for evil for supplying whatever the evil lacks in itself for drawing it about them instinctively as you do bedclothing in slumber fertilising the mind for it until the evil has served its purpose whether it ever existed or no.[6]

More examples of the same attitude appear in other novels. In describing the dietician in *Light in August* Faulkner says she possesses "a natural female infallibility for the spontaneous comprehension of evil." [7] In *Absalom, Absalom!* Faulkner makes explicit the evil which proceeds from "the female principle which existed, queenly and complete, in the hot equatorial groin of the world",[8] which causes men to possess a "dread and fear of females which you must have drawn in with the primary mammalian milk".[9] Likewise in *The Hamlet,* Eula Varner is pictured as "the supreme and primal uterus"; therefore, she is called "another mortal natural enemy of the masculine race".[10] These selected statements illustrate the extent to which Faulkner is willing to go in identifying woman as a possible source of evil in man's life and world.

Because he sees women as a constant source of evil, Faulkner displays the range of their destructive power through a variety of types – the wayward wife, the selfish mother, the adolescent sexpot, the whore, and the lustful spinster – all of whom identify so instinctively with evil they create a certainty of violence, the sign of evil. The certainty of violence is the basis for Faulkner's destructive female principle which invariably aligns, embattles, and dooms men.[11] I would like to begin the study of destructive female power by examining the wayward wife in *The Wild Palms* and proceed to the selfish mothers in *The Sound and the Fury* and *As I Lay Dying*; after that I will examine Temple Drake in *Sanctuary* as the best example of the adolescent who uses sex as

---

6   *Ibid.,* pp. 115-16.
7   *Light in August,* p. 110.
8   *Absalom, Absalom!,* p. 116.
9   *Ibid.,* p. 265.
10   *The Hamlet,* p. 114.
11   *The Wild Palms,* p. 57.

a toy, and close with an analysis of the various women in *Light in August* who bring about Joe Christmas' tragedy.

In *The Wild Palms* Faulkner uses counterpointing themes to define the nature of evil in a destructive woman and shows why it dooms men; the counterpoint highlights the contrast between two different types of women – the wayward wife and the willing mother. However, this counterpointing device has confused some readers. One of them asked Faulkner what *The Wild Palms* is about. He replied, "Two kinds of love." Of course, one of the loves is a love in name only. Faulkner explains:

The story I was trying to tell was the story of Charlotte and Harry Wilbourne [*The Wild Palms*]. I decided that it needed a contrapuntal quality like music. And so I wrote the other story [*Old Man*] simply to underline the story of Charlotte and Harry. I wrote the two stories by alternate chapters. I'd write the chapter of one and then I would write the chapter of the other just as the musician puts in – puts counterpoint behind the theme that he is working with.

The theme that Faulkner is working with in *The Wild Palms* is Charlotte and Harry's search for love and a place "where they could be lovers – to escape from the world". They are unsuccessful in their attempt, and the point of contrast between the stories is that the convict and the pregnant woman in *Old Man* "saved what Charlotte and Wilbourne had sacrificed everything to get". Faulkner further explains, "That's what I mean by counterpoint . . . that these two people had what Charlotte and Harry had given up everything – respectability, future, everything, for." Therefore, the people in *Old Man* "didn't need names, they just needed to be people in motion doing the exact opposite thing to the tragedy of Harry and Charlotte".[12] The lack of motion in Charlotte and Harry reveals their rigidity and their desire to force their design upon society. Instead of possessing a fluidity that would enable them to adapt to a situation or change, they attempt to "escape from the world" in order to keep love. It is Charlotte who refuses to adapt to the terms of life; it is she who forces her idea of love on all the others; it is she who causes the destruction of others through selfishness, carnality, and irresponsibility.

[12]   Gwynn and Blotner, *Faulkner in the University*, pp. 171, 178.

Charlotte Rittenmeyer is a woman so consumed by a romantic and sexual concept of love that it even isolates her from her lover. At first Harry thinks that Charlotte is taken with the idea of making their illicit love acceptable to society.

It's not the romance of illicit love which draws them [women] not the pasionate idea of two damned and doomed isolated forever against the world and God and the irrevocable which draws men; it's because the idea of illicit love is a challenge to them, because they have an irresistible desire to . . . take the illicit love and make it respectable.

However, Harry later discovers Charlotte does not want respectable love; she wants to keep love illicit in order to keep it passionate. Harry only slowly realizes that she is in love with love.

She grasped his hair again, hurting him again though now he knew she knew she was hurting him. "Listen: it's got to be all honeymoon, always. Forever and ever, until one of us dies. It cant be anything else. Either heaven, or hell: no comfortable safe peaceful purgatory between for you and me to wait in until good behavior or forbearance or shame or repentance overtakes us."
"So it's not me you believe in put trust in; it's love." She looked at him. "Not just me; any man."
"Yes. It's love. They say love dies between two people. That's wrong. It doesn't die. It just leaves you, goes away, if you are not good enough, worthy enough. It doesn't die; you're the one that dies."

Charlotte, therefore, wants to "burn with a hard, gem-like flame" in love, and believes that their love will not leave them if they are "good enough, strong enough". Harry eventually sees that Charlotte is so devoted to love that *"There's a part of her that doesn't love anybody, anything"*, that she is really alone, *"Why she's alone. Not lonely, alone."* [13] Charlotte is totally dedicated to fulfill herself; she feels no responsibility to anyone or anything.

The extent of Charlotte's unwillingness to accept responsibility is seen by her attitude toward her pregnancy, for she is willing to fight her pregnancy in order to keep her love "romantic" and self-directed. When she frantically seeks escape from the responsibility love implies, Charlotte begins a destructive cycle. She tries to convince Harry to perform an abortion upon her to destroy the

[13]   *The Wild Palms*, pp. 82-83.

child that threatens to invade their love. "It's not us now. That's why: don't you see? I want it to be us again, quick, quick. We have so little time. In twenty years I cant any more." [14] Harry wants to exclaim that this child would be different; "he was about to say, 'But this will be ours', when he realized that this was it, this was exactly it." [15] He senses Charlotte does not want anybody's baby; she only wants love. When she eventually forces Harry to perform the abortion, the abortion fails, Charlotte dies from an infection, and Harry is sent to prison for performing an illegal operation. Charlotte has brought about her own death and Harry's imprisonment. Her warped idea of love causes her to deny life in herself, for herself, and on behalf of others.

Charlotte has a peculiar and destructive concept of love. She aggressively seeks to realize this love and force it to come to life; because her idea of love is unreal and *contra* nature and society, there is no life in it. This is why from the beginning Harry has felt an imminent doom in the face of "the entire female principle". Charlotte makes Harry "the fool of love" because he realizes too late that he has been "seduced to an imbecile's paradise by an old whore; I have been throttled and sapped of strength and volition by the old weary Lilith of the year." [16] This, however, Charlotte does not believe and cannot accept.

Charlotte's rejection of the mother role is a typical symbol in Faulkner's novels. The gesture represents to him the worst kind of evil because it is narcissistic and irresponsible; it denies life and causes innocent children to suffer. Two of his most successful novels – *The Sound and the Fury* and *As I Lay Dying* – feature selfish mothers who deny their mother roles, creating thereby a tragedy for their families. The consequences are tragic and destructive. Cleanth Brooks has shrewdly pointed out that "what happens in *The Sound and the Fury* is to be accounted for in terms of Mrs. Compson".[17] And in *As I Lay Dying* it is easy to

[14]   *Ibid.*, p. 210.
[15]   *Ibid.*, p. 217.
[16]   *The Wild Palms*, pp. 114-15. Harry makes this remark about nature, but the parallel to Charlotte is obvious.
[17]   Brooks, "Primitivism in The Sound and the Fury", *English Institute Essays 1952* (New York, 1954), p. 14.

see that the mother, Addie Bundren, directs her family in life and death. Both of these mothers have sons whom they fail: Quentin Compson says, "if I'd just had a mother so I could say Mother Mother",[18] and Darl Bundren says, "I have no mother." [19] Both of these men are tragic casualties of a mother who rejects them and is unwilling to give a love they have a right to expect.

Mrs. Compson is a whining, selfish hypochondriac who rules the Compson home in ways that will always serve her desires best. She is aware that she is being left out of the real family life, so she develops two methods of maintaining power. She plays sick so people can attend her, and she takes a martyr's attitude toward her marriage because her husband is a man who feels his family is above hers. Mr. Compson's bitter attitude about women, already noted, and the fact that he drinks himself to death, are probably both due to Mrs. Compson. It is Mr. Compson who voices the idea of an instinctive masculine responsibility that women count upon and use for their own advantage. Still, he ironically teaches his children that "no Compson has ever disappointed a lady".[20] Quentin unthinkingly accepts this, but Mrs. Compson feels he may have forgotten the fact when he committed suicide. "What reason did Quentin have? Under God's heaven what reason did he have? It can't be simply to flout and hurt me. Whoever God is, He would not permit that. I'm a lady. You might not believe that from my offspring, but I am." [21] All of Mrs. Compson's selfishness and irresponsible unconcern are summed up in this statement. Her self-concern places her above and beyond her family, for she feels a Southern lady has certain inalienable rights that come first.

In almost every case Mrs. Compson's manipulation of her children reveals a root of self-interest. Pride forces her to change her idiot son's name from Maury, a name in her family, to Benjamin; a desire for social prestige leads her to try and marry off her daughter to a banker; and vanity is behind her desire for

[18] *The Sound and the Fury*, p. 190.
[19] *As I Lay Dying*, p. 406.
[20] *The Sound and the Fury*, p. 197.
[21] *Ibid.*, p. 315.

Quentin to attend Harvard ("that for you to go to Harvard has been your mother's dream since you were born").[22] She forces behavior upon her children to satisfy herself, and Quentin recognizes that the children have been forgotten and unloved. As he looks at a picture of a jail, he thinks, "the dungeon was Mother herself she and Father upward into weak light holding hands and us lost somewhere below even them without a ray of light".[23] Quentin further realizes that his mother's false pride poisoned the family, "because one of our forefathers was a governor and three were generals and Mother's weren't . . . *Done in Mother's mind though. Finished. Finished. Then we were all poisoned.*" [24] Mrs. Compson's manipulation is really her means of maintaining independence, but Quentin is not fooled, and neither is Jason. Her estrangement from her other children and her lack of discernment are revealed in her feelings toward Jason. Jason always uses his mother and despises her, but Mrs. Compson is unaware and says:

I'll take Jason and go where nobody knows us so he'll have a chance to grow up and forget all this, the others don't love me they have never loved anything with that streak of Compson selfishness and false pride. Jason was the only one my heart went out to without dread.[25]

The irony here, of course, is that Mrs. Compson is the one who is characterized by selfishness and false pride, and Jason is the one child who actually abuses his mother. Caroline Compson is a woman totally blinded by her all-encompassing self-interest.

Quentin and Caddy especially suffer as the results of their mother's failure. Faulkner attempts to show in *The Sound and the Fury* how Quentin's despair and Caddy's selfishness are attributable to the mother. From the very beginning Mrs. Compson has shut them out of her life. Naturally, she feels it is she who has been shut out by Quentin and Caddy, but her defensive statements reveal the fault is hers.

[22] *Ibid.*, p. 196.
[23] *Ibid.*, p. 191.
[24] *Ibid.*, p. 121.
[25] *Ibid.*

They deliberately shut me out of their lives ... They were always conspiring against me ... They always looked upon you [Jason] and me as outsiders, like they did your Uncle Maury. I always told your father that they were allowed too much freedom, to be together too much ... And then when her troubles began I knew that Quentin would feel he had to do something just as bad. But I didn't believe that he would have been so selfish as to ... But I'm just a poor old woman; I was raised to believe that people would deny themselves for their own flesh and blood.[26]

Mrs. Compson is very eager to have her children deny themselves for her, but she is never willing to take that action in their behalf. Consequently, Quentin is forced by his mother's failure toward him to look to his sister, and here again, a woman fails to give him love and guidance free from selfish motive. The result, of course, adds to his suicidal despair. Caddy does not want to fail Quentin, but her denial of him is analogous to the denial of her role as mother. With these views in mind it becomes a little easier to understand Faulkner's description of the novel as "the tragedy of two women".[27]

Mrs. Compson's influence upon Caddy is not explicitly stated in the novel, but it is clearly suggested that it is negative. Quentin always speaks for both himself and Caddy when he expresses the need of a mother. Caddy lacks a moral center to guide and control her actions; she seeks the love she needs through sex. Faulkner emphasizes that her actions are selfish too, but sympathy is aroused for her because of her mother. Quentin, therefore, is like Wilbourne; he is "aligned, embattled and doomed before the entire female principle"; his mother and his sister create needs in him they are unwilling to satisfy. His tragic suicide indicts both of the women in his family even though he bears the responsibility for his own character and his own life.

In *As I Lay Dying* Faulkner attempts to illustrate the enormous influence a powerful mother can exert upon her children. The figure of Addie Bundren is presented with intensity in order to emphasize her peculiar hold upon her family. Addie is a woman enchanted with the death wish. She is obsessively committed to

---

[26] *Ibid.*, pp. 278-79.
[27] Grenier, "Interview with William Faulkner", p. 177.

her father's teaching that "the reason for living was to get ready to stay dead a long time".[28] She believes life can only have meaning when it is piercingly defined by violent action. Therefore, Addie lives with a self-centered abandon, sacrificing herself and threatening her family through her intensive relationships. The violent action she advocates is a threat to her family because they are forced into behavior and relationships they do not choose, but Addie is so strong she makes them live life on her terms. The result is that her power destroys the family unity and brings insanity upon one of her sons.

All of Addie's actions become comprehensible when they are understood in terms of her views on life and death. Death is negation – nothing, and words symbolize the nothingness; life is positive – action. She explains active life to herself in figurative terms; she sees it as "the wild blood boiling along the earth", for in this way she visualizes the union between men's acts and nature. Addie feels she has been betrayed by marriage, for her husband is a man of meaningless words. Consequently, the birth of her first two children seems to her a violation of life. While giving birth she feels she would like to kill Anse, her husband. Addie expresses her revolt through an illicit love affair with the preacher Whitfield; he is a man of false rhetoric who drops his pretense for a moment and "sins" his way into life. Addie regards her own behavior as an expression of wild blood and the earth itself. The child she bears is precious, so she calls him Jewel. After Jewel is born Addie says, ". . . the wild blood boiled away and the sound of it ceased. Then there was only the milk, warm and calm, and I lying calm in the slow silence, getting ready to clean my house." [29] Addie has fully realized the violence of life; life is now quiescent, over; there is nothing more to live for.

Despite the fact that she has achieved a goal in life, Addie refuses to integrate her children into her life. Her initial attitude toward Darl eventually becomes her typical attitude toward the whole family. From the very beginning Darl has been an unwanted child. Addie grudgingly accepts her first son, Cash, as the

[28]   *As I Lay Dying*, p. 461.
[29]   *Ibid.*, p. 467.

price of her marriage, and she accepts Jewel and loves him because he represents active life; her last two children she employs
as "gifts" to her husband in order to atone for Jewel. Darl does
not fit into her life at all. It is he who correctly senses, "I have
no mother." [30] He is forced to live in a family where his existence
does not count; as a result he is a little "queer". The moment
she feels she has gained all that life can offer her, Addie treats the
rest of her children with the same cold indifference she displays
toward Darl. The children react accordingly; Dewey Dell attempts to find love in sex; she is seduced and bears an unwanted
child she tries to abort – the symbol of evil, a denial of motherhood, is present again – and the youngest son, Vardaman, is so
confused by his mother's indifference and eventual death, that
he associates his mother with a dying fish. ("My Mother is a
fish." [31]) In time Addie drops her husband and four of her children out of her life because they no longer serve her purpose. For
Darl this means madness, for the others confusion, suffering and
eventual dissolution.

Even when she is dead, Addie manipulates her family to her
advantage. Her wish to be buried in Jefferson forces the family
on a ritualistic journey through flood and fire to fulfill a seeming-
ly capricious desire. The journey exerts a great toll upon all the
family. Cash breaks a leg, the family wagon and goods are lost,
another wagon is burned up, and Dewey Dell is seduced again
and robbed. The final dissolution of the family is symbolized by
the way they all turn against Darl. Darl tries to end the ritualistic
journey by setting fire to a barn that holds his mother's coffin.
The children exhibit the mother's dominion by risking life in
order to save her. After the fire they begin to plot against Darl.
When they arrive in Jefferson, they seize him and send him off
to the state insane asylum. Once again an irony is apparent; Darl
is the only child who sees through his mother and his bastard
brother, Jewel, yet it is he who is judged insane. Addie is powerful enough in life and death to prevent Darl from succeeding in

[30]   *Ibid.*, p. 406.
[31]   *Ibid.*, p. 398.

righteous protest. She gets what she wants, but she fails as a mother and destroys her family in order to achieve it.

Most of the critics have recognized the importance of Mrs. Compson and Addie Bundren to the tragedies of their families, but none, so far as I know, explains their relation to the tragedy in terms of their roles as mothers. Yet this role explains their power. Mrs. Vickery notes that Mrs. Compson abandons her "humanity for the sake of pride or vanity or self pity",[32] but she does not explain how these characteristics, combined with her role as mother, produce the tragic action. We have shown how Quentin regards his mother's attitude as the "poison" that later brings his lament, "If I only had a mother." Quentin is as much a victim of his mother and sister as he is of his father. Another critic observed of *As I Lay Dying* that Addie "is a proud and bitter woman and that she as much as anything else is responsible for the hatred and pain within the Bundren family".[33] And Waggoner also notes of Addie that her rejection of her children parallels Captain Ahab's rejection of the request of the captain of the *Rachael*.[34] These two observations are correct as far as they go, but it must be noted that Faulkner is illustrating the destructive power of woman through her most important role. Addie and Mrs. Compson are central to the novels because the tragedy of their children originates with them.

Mrs. Compson and Addie Bundren are both intensely selfish mothers who traffic with the emotions and needs of their children in order to feed their own needs for self-realization. This is their evil: their children need them, but they reject them and use the children as things. The children become tragic victims of their mothers' erratic behavior, for they are not as great as their needs for mother love. Faulkner uses the mother role to illustrate again that sexually irresponsible women like Addie and Mrs. Compson, are evil; they energize a destructive female principle.[35]

---

[32] Vickery, *The Novels of William Faulkner*, p. 47.
[33] Slatoff, *Quest for Failure*, p. 164.
[34] Waggoner, *From Jefferson to the World*, p. 82.
[35] Faulkner uses the symbolic rejection of the mother role again in *Requiem for a Nun*. When Temple is about to abandon her child and run

Another type of female who can exert destructive power is the adolescent who plays with sex and men as with a toy. In his first two novels, *Soldier's Pay* and *Mosquitoes*, Faulkner begins to develop this type. The adolescent in *Soldier's Pay* is Cecily Saunders; in *Mosquitoes* it is Patricia Robyn. Faulkner pictures them as "epicene" teen-agers who have "two little knobs for breasts and indicated buttocks that, except for their soft look, might belong to a boy of fifteen".[36] They are intense and nervous about their sex roles, trying to figure out the relationships between love, sex, marriage and children. Faulkner describes Cecily in bed:

... running her fingers lightly over her breasts, across her belly, drawing concentric circles upon her body beneath the covers, wondering how it would feel to have a baby, hating that inevitable time when she'd have to have one, blurring her slim epicenity, blurring her body with pain.[37]

Cecily's apprehensiveness of the mother role is a clear forecast of her irresponsible sexuality; subsequently, she plunges into a purely carnal affair with the town lover deserting her wounded fiance. Patricia Robyn entices a young man to elope with her and then drops him when they cannot get to a justice of the peace. Thus Faulkner illustrates in his early works the power young girls possess because of sex and begins to work toward the idea of a tragedy created through immature sexual irresponsibility.

In *Sanctuary* Faulkner brings the sexually irresponsible adolescent into full realization in the character of Temple Drake. As the novel opens Temple is seventeen years old, a popular coed at Ole Miss, living a life of respectable promiscuity. As the novel closes Temple's sexual irresponsibility has characterized the evil condition of the world itself:

---

off with Red, Nancy steps in and slays the child to prevent the abandonment. This is a bizarre use of the symbol but indicates again the depth of evil it represents to Faulkner. The little child is the innocent victim, and Stevens states one of the main themes of the drama when he says that adults must be willing to suffer so that the little children of the world may come to "Him" without anguish and unafraid. This suffering is a step along the road to salvation. See *Requiem for a Nun*, pp. 162-63.

36 *Mosquitoes*, p. 240.
37 *Soldier's Pay*, pp. 142-43.

She closed the compact and from beneath her smart new hat she
seemed to follow with her eyes the waves of music, to dissolve into
the dying brasses, across the pool and the opposite semicircle of trees
where at sombre intervals the dead tranquil queens in stained marble
mused, and on into the sky lying prone and vanquished in the em-
brace of the season of rain and death.[38]

Sanctuary is the brutal record of a flippant and heedless child
whose very behavior creates and characterizes her time as "the
season of rain and death".

Temple is archly provocative, a trait that is respected and even
admired on the college campus, but when she attempts the same
type of behavior in a moonshiner's cabin, she creates an explosive
chain reaction. The college boys know her game and play along
with it, but the hardened criminals translate her flirtatious invita-
tions into sexual violence. Temple is not unaware of her danger,
but this only intensifies the experience for her. She is using her
sexual promise as a means to explore the danger. In the moonshiner's cabin Mrs. Godwin recognizes that she is playing the
bitch and warns her that she is likely to stir up trouble. Temple
does not stop but arouses all the men, even impotent Popeye;
however, she is coy because she does not want to be held account-
able for her acts. Temple wants to be a victim in order to know
evil, yet she wishes to avoid responsibility. One observer has well
described her paradoxical desire for evil and innocence.

For only by becoming the victim of violence can she participate in
[an evil] world without losing her position in her own. Since she
does not will her rape, but only passively suffers it, she is freed
of responsibility for it, thus enabling her to preserve her social innocence no matter what physical or moral degradation she experiences.[39]

Temple reveals her eagerness to experience evil by primping before her violation: she combs her hair and freshens her make-up.
She seeks the violation as a means of gratification, and though it
appears she is a victim, she actually victimizes everyone else
through her behavior. Thus Godwin loses his life for a murder he

---

[38] *Sanctuary*, p. 380.
[39] Vickery, *The Novels of William Faulkner*, pp. 107-08.

did not commit; the lawyer, Benbow, loses his faith in justice; and Ruby Godwin loses her husband. But Temple emerges intact, still putting on her make up, in a world she proves is evil.

Faulkner shows how Temple's sexual irresponsibility eventually degenerates into total corruption – time and again she refuses to run away from danger and evil. She can run away at the cabin, at the filling station, or at Miss Reba's, but by being a willful prisoner, she can continue to be sexually "victimized". Toward the end of her experience she loses every trace of restraint or pretense. She plays the complete bitch with Red just before Popeye kills him out of jealousy.

He came toward her. She did not move. Her eyes began to grow darker and darker, lifting into her skull above a half moon of white, without focus, with the blank rigidity of a statue's eyes. She began to say Ah-ah-ah-ah in an expiring voice, her body arching slowly backward as though forced by an exquisite torture. When he touched her she sprang like a bow, hurling herself upon him, her mouth gaped and ugly like that of a dying fish as she writhed her loins against him ... with her hips grinding against him, her mouth gaping on straining protrusion, bloodless, she began to speak. "Let's hurry. Anywhere ... Come on. What're you waiting for?' She strained her mouth toward him, dragging his head down, making a whimpering moan ... "Please, please. Please. Please. Don't make me wait. I'm burning up.[40]

Leslie Fiedler regards Temple's lust as "the ultimate desecration, the total denial of the archetype of the ethereal virgin". To Fiedler Temple's corruption is the desecration of "a cult object" (the Young Girl, the Heiress of the Ages) but more important, he correctly notes that Temple's total corruption has turned her into destructive force – "the Fair Maiden has become the rapist", for Red represents to Temple "sexuality detached from responsibility, impulse without mind"; he is to her both thug and stud, and she uses him to continue the "rape". When Red is killed, Temple is sad because "it will never be again".[41] Later when she is on the stand and can save the innocent Godwin, Temple is so degenerated she lies for no obvious reason and sends an innocent man to his death. Temple's total corruption is another evidence

---

[40] *Sanctuary*, pp. 277-78.
[41] Fiedler, *Love and Death in the American Novel*, pp. 311-12.

that her moral awareness has been lost within her female carnality; thus she gains a "natural affinity for evil". Her alliance with evil, therefore, is definitive because it has gained control of her nature. She hardens from the provocative sexpot into the degenerate bitch, and her capacity for inhuman and destructive acts grows as her capacity for love and responsibility diminishes.

It is possible that the title of this novel may be an ironic comment on contemporary woman. In the Middle Ages a person could escape being jailed or persecuted by seeking sanctuary in a church, for the church as "mother" receives and protects its "children". Temple, as her name might indicate, is a potential refuge, but because of her carnality, her spiritual resources to receive or protect are non-existent. Therefore, the Young Maiden, the heiress of the ages, the cult object of the modern age, in short, the woman who can be a sanctuary to man brings death instead of life because she chooses sex instead of love. Instead of being loved by men to her fulfillment and their good, Temple uses men for a carnal self-gratification.

Up to this point we have considered Charlotte Rittenmeyer, Mrs. Compson, Addie Bundren, and Temple Drake as women who possess destructive power because the roles they play as women give them control over men and children. The men and children in their lives need them and feel instinctive responsibility to satisfy or obey them. These women are irresponsible to the needs they create. We have seen the tragedy that results from such evil acts. These women not only do evil, they *are* evil to Faulkner, and the behavioral signs of their evil are carnality and irresponsibility. We now turn to *Light in August* for the strongest exposition of this theme. The intensity of this novel is derived from the successive encounters of Joe Christmas with destructive females and his persistent tendency to interpret the nature of life itself by the nature of woman. The repetition of the theme of destructive female power in an ontological context makes *Light in August* Faulkner's best exposition of the malignant power of sexual irresponsibility.

The familiar evil of a woman using man selfishly and sexually appears repeatedly in the novel. Joe Christmas has a series of

relationships with women who use him in order that they may
gratify personal and social ambitions. They refuse to let Joe be an
individual – a human being; they classify and categorize him in
order to use him. These women represent but one of the forces
that encircle Christmas. It does not matter to these women, or
the other forces in society that victimize Joe, that this social definition as Negro may be wrong; it only matters that a definition
be made in order that life may be lived in its accustomed pattern.
The women who help destroy Joe Christmas are blind to anything
but an aggressive self-fulfillment which makes them, in Faulkner's view, enemies of man.

Joe Christmas' birth and early experiences set a pattern of how
he is to be abused and misled by women. Joe's mother abandons
him on the doorstep of a brothel on Christmas Eve. This abandonment – a rejection of the mother role – plants the seed of evil in
his life. It makes him "the poor little Jesus boy" his name suggests who lives in a world where "they didn't know who you
was". In the brothel – itself a symbol of sexual irresponsibility
and rejected motherhood – he is a bawdy joke. The madam takes
Joe where he belongs: to an orphanage. At the orphanage Joe's
grandfather transmits his misinformation about Joe to the dietician who uses it in a moment of crisis because she possesses a
"natural female infallibility for the comprehension of evil". Joe
accidentally gets hidden in a room where the dietician makes love.
He has no idea of what goes on, but the woman goes out of her
head with fear. A fiendish insight serves to provide her with an
abusive plan: she will get Joe out of the white orphanage by ac-
cusing him of being a Negro. This idea of his being a Negro is a
convenient tool and she now calls him a "nigger bastard", and

... she believed that she had, had known it all the while, because it
seemed so right: he would not only be removed; he would be punished
for having given her terror and worry.[42]

The dietician is able to get rid of Joe, but only after she has left
an indelible memory upon him. Her early attempts to buy Joe into
silence confuse him; he senses he should punished for some

42 *Light in August*, p. 113.

wrong. He wants justice from her, but gets bribery and hatred; consequently, he is very confused. These early events set the pattern of his life, and Joe's obdurate quest to know if he is black or white and his desire for judgment and not mercy characterize him until he dies. Faulkner stresses the melancholy fact that Joe's memory had recorded these events, and the style of the description indicates the bleak prospect for his life.

Memory believes before knowing remembers. Believes longer than recollects, longer than knowing even wonders. Knows remembers believes a corridor in a big long garbled cold echoing building of dark red brick soot-bleakened by more chimneys than its own . . . the bleak windows where in rain soot from the yearly adjacenting chimneys streaked like black tears.[43]

When Joe is a growing boy he is very unsure about the nature of women and the need he feels for them. As an isolated farm boy he sees girls "only at church, on Sunday. They were associated with Sunday and with church. So he could not notice them." About this time an older boy offers him an explanation about the nature of women: "They all want to . . . But sometimes they can't . . . It's something that happens to them once a month." Then the boy describes "his idea of the physical ceremony":

He drew a picture, physical, actual, to be discerned by the sense of smell and even of sight. It moved them: the temporary and abject helplessness of that which tantalised and frustrated desire; the smooth and superior shape in which volition dwelled doomed to be at stated and inescapable intervals victims of periodical filth. That was how the boy told it, with the other five listening intently, looking at one another, questioning and secret.

Joe is utterly revolted by this revelation of "periodical filth". He fights accepting it and feels the need of a personal cleansing. A week later the feeling is still with him so he makes a gesture of protest and cleansing by killing a sheep and touching the blood.

Then he knelt, his hands in the yet warm blood of the dying beast, trembling, drymouthed, backglaring. Then he got over it, recovered.

[43] Ibid., p. 104.

Joe is still bewildered and ignorant about the nature of woman, but now, at least, he feels a measure of relief. He finds the best thing is to accept the mystery as a part of life, but he plans to avoid women for himself.

He just accepted it. He found that he could live with it side by side with it. It was as if he said, illogical and desperately calm *Allright. It is so, then. But not to me. Not in my life and my love.*[44]

Joe wants to accept woman – love – but he cannot reconcile his need with their "sickness" which seems to him a sign of uncleanliness, of evil.

Joe lives with a confused idea of woman which stays submerged in his mind until he meets the prostitute, Bobbie Allen. After something like a courtship, he lets her know he feels a physical need. Joe does not understand why she cannot make love to him; she explains, "Listen, I'm sick tonight. He did not understand." In the interval of time Joe forgot about woman's sickness.

He had forgot about the shot sheep. He had lived with the fact which the older boy had told him too long now. With the slain sheep he had bought immunity from it for too long now for it to be alive. So he could not understand at first what she was trying to tell him.

Bobbie tells him again, and Joe understands now and feels thwarted and cheated. What was resentment now becomes rage. As Faulkner says, "he had been not hurt or astonished so much as outraged". Joe is frustrated because he does not know what to do. Once again he seeks a ritualistic cleansing through nature. He runs away from Bobbie to the woods:

He reached the woods and entered, among the hard trunks, the branchshadowed quiet, hardfeeling, hardsmelling, invisible. In the notseeing and the hardknowing as though in a cave he seemed to see a diminishing row of suavely shaped urns in moonlight, blanched. And not one was perfect. Each one was cracked and from each crack there issued something liquid, deathcolored, and foul. He touched a tree, leaning his propped arms against it, seeing the ranked and moonlit urns. He vomited.[45]

---

[44] *Ibid.*, pp. 160-62.
[45] *Ibid.*, pp. 163-65.

Joe's distorted vision of the urns represents his distorted picture of woman; both nature and woman seem imperfect and foul. He does not find the cleansing he seeks. He has a need for more than ritual now. A week later he drags Bobbie to the spot in the woods and makes violent love to her. Despite his lack of understanding about woman, Joe makes an unconditional surrender to his needs and blindly places himself in the hands of a whore. He still has no understanding of woman, but he attempts to comprehend through faith. He is willing to trust love despite his ignorance.

Joe attempts to act in love and loyalty toward Bobbie, but he is unaware that she is merely tolerating him. In a moment of crisis she uses him to save herself. When Joe's stepfather attempts to separate them at a dance, Joe clubs him with a chair, then runs home and robs him. His plan is to take the money so that he and Bobbie can run away and get married. When he arrives at her place, he finds her friends already there: "I came to get Bobbie. Do you think that I – when I went all the way home to get the money to get married." When he gives Bobbie the money, she flings it away and he is incredulous: " 'You mean you wont?' he said. 'You mean you wont?' " Joe doesn't realize that he is now a threat to Bobbie because he may have killed his stepfather. Earlier Bobbie had simply passed over Joe's open statement, "I think I got some nigger blood in me"; now she finds it convenient to use this fact. "Bastard! Son of a bitch! Getting me into a jam, that always treated you like you were a white man. A white man!" Joe feels completely betrayed, "saying in a slow amazement: *Why I committed murder for her. I even stole for her.*" Bobbie's companions urge her to leave before the police come; she makes her departure from Joe easier by using Joe's own confidences as a tool: "He told me himself he was a nigger! The son of a bitch . . . a nigger son of a bitch that would get me in a jam with clodhopper police." [46] This betrayal by a woman is the final blow to Joe's attempts to find peace through love. Mrs. Vickery notes this fact and says:

Bobbie's later shrieks of rage signal the destruction of the last of Joe's natural spontaneous emotions. Her betrayal, which impels him into

[46]   *Ibid.*, pp. 188-90.

the long, lonely street of his life, is not only sexual but religious and racial, for all three are involved in the idea of miscegenation into which their affair is suddenly transformed.[47]

Bobbie's action confirms the "outrage" that Joe feels is latent in the female nature; her desertion confirms the evil and hostility of the world. He becomes now the world's antagonist, and he stalks in bitterness through the forms of social behavior, seeking avenues to vent his rage.

Joe's next encounter with woman is through Joanna Burden. Once again he is betrayed; once again he is used as an object; once again he protests and the form his protest takes is murder. The final outrage has brought on the ultimate response. Miss Burden is an abolitionist spinster who believes it is the duty of the white race to save the black. She believes that Negroes are: "doomed and cursed to be forever and ever a part of the white race's doom and curse for its sins . . . The curse of every white child that ever was born and that ever will be born." [48] When Joe comes into her life she sees him as a means of salvation – spiritual and sexual. Her duty is to lift "the black cross", so Joe becomes the symbol of her responsibility and her salvation. However, she is a sex-starved woman, as well as an aspiring saint, so she uses Joe to satisfy her physical appetite until she is satiated; only then does she repent; only then does she demand that he be Negro, that he pray and repent of *his* "sin", that he go away to a Negro college and lift himself in order that she see salvation. Miss Burden's repentance, it should be noted, is made somewhat easier, for she enters the menopause and her sexual appetite diminishes. Joe, however, senses an outrage at being tricked and used by a woman "whose very body reveals a subterfuge":

Perhaps that is where the outrage lies. Perhaps I believe that I have been tricked, fooled. That she lied to me about her age, about what happens to women at a certain age.[49]

He is so disturbed by Miss Burden's mad display of sex and her rigid desire for salvation, he begins another pattern of flight

[47] Vickery, *The Novels of William Faulkner*, p. 71.
[48] *Light in August*, p. 221.
[49] *Ibid.*, pp. 92-93.

which reveals his desire to escape from an evil world that is characterized by evil women. Peculiarly enough, the first place he
runs to is a stable.

About three hundred yards away the stable stood. It was falling down
and there had not been a horse in it in thirty years, yet it was toward
the stable that he went. He was walking quite fast. He was thinking
now, aloud now, "Why in hell do I want to smell horses?" Then he
said, fumbling: "It's because they are not women. Even a mare horse
is a kind of man." [50]

Joe continues his flight through the Negro section of town, and
coming upon a group of Negro women, he again experiences the
trapped feeling that a woman arouses in him.

On all sides, even within him, the bodiless fecund-mellow voices of
Negro women murmured. It was as though he and all other man-
shaped life about him had been returned to the lightless hot wet primogenitive Female. He began to run . . .[51]

To Joe the individually corrupt women he has known signify a
selfishly absorbing and destructive "primogenitive Female",
which in turn suggests the destructive introversion of the social
order. Joe is running to escape, but his tragedy – and one of the
tragedies of mankind Faulkner suggests – is that there is no place
to run; there is no escape from the need that a woman promises to
fulfill. As Geismar says, "Christmas is caught and then destroyed by the female, 'like a man being sucked down into a bottom-
less abyss' . . . There is indeed no redemption. Only as in *Light in
August* the continuing sense of destruction, the incessant breeding
of evil by evil [sic.]." [52]

Joe's real problem with women is that they are a promise and a
threat at the same time, and in a moment of crisis (the dietician's
discovery, Bobbie Allen's danger, Joanna Burden's fear of losing
a means to salvation) their real nature is uncovered and they are
all threat and no promise. When Joe first sees Miss Burden he
sees:

[50] *Ibid.*, p. 95.
[51] *Ibid.*, p. 100.
[52] Geismar, *Writers in Crisis*, p. 167.

A dual personality: the one the woman at first sight of whom in the lifted candle ... there had opened before him, instantaneous as a landscape in a lightningflash, a horizon of physical security and adultery if not pleasure; the other the mantrained muscles and mantrained habit of thinking born of heritage and environment with which he had to fight up to the final instant.[53]

Even a woman like Joanna Burden can become an "horizon of physical security", but unfortunately she always acts in accordance with her selfish desires. She satisfies needs of body and soul through him, and if he resists her, she is willing to kill him. She attempts to force her will upon him with a pistol, for she senses his unwillingness to seek "repentance" through prayer. Joe is expected to "ignore his own uncertainty, admit his black blood, his sinfulness, and his dependence for salvation on her and her God".[54] In other words, Joe is expected to assent to her whether or not he denies himself. This is when woman becomes most destructive – when she forces upon man a condition contrary to his nature. Joe is forced to slay Joanna Burden to vindicate his humanity and reality as a being. Her death is Faulkner's grimmest way of picturing the tragic recompense of a loveless and selfish female carnality.

In summarizing this discussion of the "female principle" we note, first of all, that in Faulkner's tragic view of life the principle postulates a law of destruction. In all but one of his tragic novels (*Absalom, Absalom!*) a woman hastens or causes the tragedy of a man through irresponsible and selfish sexuality. Of the nine woman referred to in this chapter, eight of them (Mrs. Compson excepted) use a sexual relationship with a man to fortify their own desires in life, and do so unmindful of the consequences such action may bring upon others. This type of behavior amounts to a separation of love and sex.

In his very early fiction Faulkner comments that sex can give meaning to life when it is an expression of love; however, if love is absent, sex is associated with death. In *Mosquitoes* (1927) he reveals his hope of life through sex, for in this novel he states that

---

[53] *Light in August*, p. 205.
[54] Vickery, *The Novels of William Faulkner*, p. 76.

human relationships constitute a "blank wall on which sex casts a shadow, and the shadow is life".[55] But in *Soldier's Pay* (1927) he reveals the tragic alternative when he states, "Sex and death: the front door and the back door of the world. How indissolubly are they associated in us." [56] Faulkner uses the women in his tragic novels to dramatize this indissoluble association of sex and death, and the loveless sexuality in the lives of these women suggests a larger disorder in all of life. By way of illustrating this correspondence we have seen how selfish mothers indicate an insecure basis for the whole of family life; adolescent promiscuity suggests the absence of social standards to inform and guide the young; and lusting wayward wives and spinsters exhibit animal appetites that characterize a debased human nature. In the social setting where these conditions prevail, sex is invariably associated with death, and the result is tragedy.

Part of woman's problem seems to be that she has lost a fixed role in modern society that can reveal and channel her nature. When she is cut off from the "immemorial earth", woman's source of instinctive moral power is lost. She lacks a shaping moral vision that directs her to seek creative responsibility and integrates her desires for sex, love, and freedom. Her lack of alliance with the immemorial earth severs her from the creative forces in nature, and she loses a knowledge of the end which contains and directs sex. Furthermore, she fails to learn loyalty because she has lost a trust in nature's way. Consequently, the destructive female in Faulkner's fiction is the dispossessed heiress. She has traded her birthright – an alliance with nature – for a mess of pottage. She has gained freedom but lost love; she has gained the world but lost the earth. Woman cannot be woman and bear these losses; she becomes instead a cunning and impersonal destructive female principle.

[55] *Mosquitoes*, p. 231.

[56] *Soldier's Pay*, p. 295.

IV. MOTHER LOVE

I waited not for light but for that doom which
we call female victory which is: endure and
then endure, without rhyme or reason or hope
of reward – and then endure.[1]

Absalom, Absalom!

Writing in 1952 on "The Fictional American Woman", Margrit
Reiner remarks that "the 'good woman' in fiction is the woman
happily confined in . . . 'her proper sphere'. *Love* not labor is a
woman's concern and woman's place is in the home." [2] It might
surprise a lot of people to know that this statement describes with
precision Faulkner's point of view. He has clear-cut ideas that a
woman's "proper sphere" is not the masculine world, ruled as
it is by barter and abstraction. Her sphere is "the immemorial
earth"; her concern is to love; her function is to bear her children
in serene trust; her responsibility is to love them, care for them,
and inform them of the very mystery of life. Within her sphere
woman is fecund, like the earth itself. Eula Varner is described in
just this way in *The Hamlet;* she is like "the fine land rich and
fecund and foul and eternal and impervious".[3] And the earth is
specifically called "mare to the stallion sun" a number of times.
Benbow, the defeated aristocrat in *Sanctuary*, also associates
woman's fecundity with the earth and thinks at one point:
"That's why we know nature is a she; because of that conspiracy
between female flesh and female season . . . That's why nature is

---

[1] *Absalom, Absalom!*, p. 144.
[2] Margrit Reiner, "The Fictional American Woman", *Masses and Mainstream*, VI (June 1952), p. 2.
[3] *The Hamlet*, p. 119.

'she' and Progress is 'he'; nature made the grape arbor, but Progress invented the mirror." [4] Faulkner believes that the female who completely accepts this union with nature gains knowledge and instinctive wisdom which men need and desire desperately. For instance, LaBove, the monk-faun-scholar in *The Hamlet* senses in woman a mysterious superiority and indicates the extent to which he will go to know what she knows.

> It would now be himself importunate and prostrate before that face which, even though but fourteen years old, postulated a weary knowledge which he would never attain, a surfeit, a glut of all perverse experience. He would be as a child before that knowledge. He would be like a young girl, a maiden, wild distracted and amazed, trapped not by the seducer's maturity and experience but by blind and ruthless forces inside herself which she now realized she had lived with for years without even knowing they were there. He would grovel in the dust before it, panting: "Show me what to do. Tell me. I will do anything you tell me, anything, to learn and know what you know." [5]

What a fourteen-year-old woman possesses is the mystery of life as a creative force. Woman in her sphere, therefore, is a part and parcel of nature in ways not given to man; the creative life force permeates the whole egg of life, including woman. Her acceptance of herself as receptacle of life gives her security because she knows herself and wisdom because she remains open to knowledge through others. By accepting herself she becomes free to love others. Faulkner feels, therefore, that love, children, and the home become the defining ends she serves. And since she is characterized by love, she is godlike. This is why Faulkner refers to the "good" woman in "her proper sphere" as the "Passive and Anonymous whom God had created to be not alone the recipient and receptacle of the seed of his body but of his spirit too, which is truth". [6]

The use of the word "anonymous" in describing a good woman immediately calls to mind Ike McCaslin's phrase, "the communal anonymity of brotherhood". And, of course, the point of comparison is that woman's role as life bearer provides her with an op-

[4] *Sanctuary*, pp. 13, 16.
[5] *The Hamlet*, p. 120.
[6] *Light in August*, pp. 408-09.

portunity to learn selflessness. Man must learn or acquire this truth from Nature. He may even learn it from nature's prime specimen of life – woman, Eve – and this is easiest and best. But woman is vouchsafed anonymity through the role of motherhood, for motherhood provides her a vehicle for the continuing exhibition of responsible selflessness. As we have shown, in Faulkner's fiction the woman who denies motherhood denies life, for this denial is motivated by an individualistic assertion of ego. Passivity and anonymity are rejected by wayward wives, selfish mothers, adolescent sexpots, lustful spinsters. They are malignant within the chain of life; they challenge and threaten brotherhood and the community of man. What is just as bad is that they are ignorant, and men who believe they "know", who fall into their power seeking a meaning to life, are destroyed. But when woman willingly fulfills the function of her existence through motherhood, she affirms life in herself and others. She is Eve in the garden in full possession of the earth. Through motherhood, she eliminates the curse; Eden is reclaimed, she is the "heiress of all the ages", because she exhibits "a moral vision" that can, in the words of Wasserstrom "integrate and unify [society's] three leading preoccupations – sex, love, and freedom".[7]

There are not many "good" women in Faulkner's fiction; as a matter of fact, there is no one woman who is seen to adequately perform all the functions of responsible motherhood – birth, care, and education. The reason for this seems apparent. Faulkner does not believe our society produces a responsible type of woman. Modern woman is cut off from the earth and suffers the consequences; the socially oriented woman in his view is as typically individualistic and mercenary as the Snopeses. However, there are some women in his fiction who perform one or more of the functions of responsible womanhood, and by examining each of these women separately, we can come to see the qualities that characterize the ideal woman. The first figure we will examine is the earth mother. Women like Lena Grove in *Light in August* and the pregnant woman in *The Wild Palms* represent this type. Secondly, we will look at the foster mother; Dilsey stands alone

7   Wasserstrom, *Heiress of All the Ages*, p. viii.

here. Finally, we will consider the grandmother figure, "granny".
Aunt Jenny Du Pre in *Sartoris,* Rosa Millard in *The Unvanquished* and Miss Habersham in *Intruder in the Dust* are women of this
mold. It should be noted that the foster mother and the grandmother are really mother surrogates, which is a clear indication
that Faulkner thinks mother love is not characteristic of our time.
One other thing worth observing is that each of these mothers
performs a separate function within the range of a mother's responsibilities: the earth mother gives birth in loving fulfillment of
her nature; the foster mother cares for the infant in protective
love; the grandmother informs the youth of "truth". This frag-
mentation of the ideal, whole woman is worth putting together,
for it presents another facet of a typical characterization in
Faulkner's late fiction – a creative individual, such as the corporal in *A Fable* or Gavin Stevens in *Snopes*, who is informed by
nature, and who acts on behalf of mankind.

The earth mother is a figure in Faulkner's fiction that has had
some little development. She is anticipated in an early essay that
he wrote for the *New Orleans Times – Picayune*. The piece for
the newspaper is entitled "Out of Nazareth", a title which suggests that the serene belief and trust of a pregnant woman is a
religious state. A young man on the open road is assigned characteristics which clearly indicate that Faulkner had already con-
ceived of the earth mother as a definite character by 1925.

He reminded one of a pregnant woman in his calm belief that nature,
the earth which had spawned him, would care for him, that he was
serving his appointed ends, had served his appointed end and now
need only wait. For what? He had probably never thought of it. As
all simple children of the earth know, he knew that even poverty
would take care of its own.[8]

In addition to this seed of an idea, many of Faulkner's earlier
novels picture potential earth mothers as young girls who listen
to the message of nature through their developing bodies. Zink
regards these musing maidens (Belle Benbow of *Sanctuary*, Judith
Sutpen of *Absalom, Absalom!* Cecily Saunders of *Soldier's Pay,*

[8]   *New Orleans Sketches*, p. 103.

and Eula Varner of *The Hamlet*) "as strange paradoxes of apparent spirituality and frankest physicality ... This is the young girl who, for a magical time between puberty and full maturity, exists in an oblivious state of listening bemusement which relates directly to the obliviousness of Nature." [9] This state of maidenhood is a transition stage between childhood and womanhood – a stage in which the female is conscious of her own maturation, receiving thereby a message containing the secret of life. Faulkner says in *Absalom, Absalom!* that this is a condition in which

... young girls appear as though seen through glass and where even the voice cannot reach them ... where they exist ... in a pearly lambence without shadows and themselves partaking of it; in nebulous suspension held, strange and unpredictable, even their very shapes fluid and delicate and without substance; not in themselves floating and seeking but merely waiting, parasitic and potent and serene.[10]

Eula Varner in *The Hamlet* is depicted in the same state:

She seemed to be not a living integer of her contemporary scene, but rather to exist in a teeming vacuum in which her days followed one another as though behind sound-proof glass, where she seemed to listen in sullen bemusement, with a weary wisdom heired of all mammalian maturity, to the enlarging of her own organs.[11]

Thus from the early pictures of the simple earth child and the musing maiden, we can see that Faulkner's interest in the earth mother has a significant history. Furthermore, we can note two constituent elements in her make up: spiritual trust and organic isolation. These two qualities are the prime ingredients in the character of Lena Grove, Faulkner's best illustration of this type.

As the novel *Light in August* opens, Lena Grove, pregnant, is on a quiet, relentless search for her seducer, Lucas Burch. As the novel closes Lena, her child born, continues on her way still searching for the child's father. Between her arrival and departure in Jefferson, violence erupts in the form of murder and lynching, but Lena's quiet presence and serene trust, plus her seeming help-

---

[9] Zink, "Faulkner's Garden: Woman and the Immemorial Earth", *Modern Fiction Studies*, II (Autumn 1956),p. 144.
[10] *Absalom, Absalom!*, p. 67.
[11] *The Hamlet*, p. 195.

lessness, has inspired some of the men who meet her to responsible and renewing action. Wasserstrom sees Lena as capable of
unifying love, sex and freedom, and, furthermore, he is of the
firm opinion that "until very recently, Faulkner was the only
novelist to organize all [these] traditional elements in a single
moral vision. But his best opinion of love – illustrated by Lena
in *Light in August* – is that it is motivated by an impulse to
maternality. And this is not an adequate view of its complexity
or power." [12] Wasserstrom misses the figurative significance of
Lena's maternality that Malin picks up when he observes, "I
believe that the state of motherhood is symbolic throughout the
novel [because] her physical condition . . . is indicative of the too
easily forgotten fecundity of nature." [13] Malin's point is very clear,
for Lena's maternity supplies her with all that nature can offer;
therefore, her love – maternal as it might be – is adequate in her
situation. Through love Lena endures, inspires, and saves life –
her own, her child's, and her man's. Mr. Wasserstrom may be
quite right if he believes that maternity as a complete definition
of love is inadequate for our age, but I think he would have to see
that the maternal definition of love is adequate for the novel. In
Faulkner's world mother love is complex and powerful enough to
supply all the demands of intrapersonal and intersexual relationships that he wishes to picture.

Lena's union with nature is specifically developed in ways
suggesting her as timeless, beautiful, and spiritual. Faulkner bor-
rows an image from Keats to describe her pilgrimage and evoke a
truth-beauty association. Lena is like "something moving forever and without progress across an urn",[14] and her timeless endurance is that of nature itself: "She went out of sight up the
road: swollen, slow, deliberate, unhurried and tireless as aug-
menting afternoon itself." [15] However, it is as Lena experiences
the premature pains of childbirth that she makes a response identifying her as earth's own simple child. When she is gripped by a

[12] Wasserstrom, *Heiress of All the Ages*, p. 104.
[13] Malin, *William Faulkner*, p. 44.
[14] *Light in August*, p. 6.
[15] *Ibid.*, p. 9.

labor pain, Lena is "waging a mild battle with that providential caution of the old earth of and with and by which she lives".[16] Later another spasm seizes her, but Lena is unafraid because she is in "her proper sphere": "Her face has drained of color, of its full, hearty blood, and she sits quite still, hearing and feeling the implacable and immemorial earth, but without fear or alarm." [17] Lena is a picture of the creative female fully defined by her role as life bearer.

Lena's creative and renewing power is felt by many people in the novel (like the Armstids and Byron Bunch), but she has the most profound effect upon the recluse Hightower, because he is forced to deliver her baby. Before the baby comes Hightower hears Lena speaking while in the throes of labor. It is an unrecognizable earth language unknown to man that clearly identifies Lena as woman.

It was a moaning wail, loud, with a quality at once passionate and abject, that seemed to be speaking clearly to something in a tongue which he knew was not his tongue nor that of any man.[18]

He is unnerved at first but then calmed; he delivers the baby because life gives him no choice. The immunity he sought, that isolation from life, is broken by the action: he immediately feels "a glow, a wave, a surge of something almost hot, almost triumphant". For a moment he feels free from the dead past; "I have surrendered too", he thinks, and he means surrendered to life as Lena has done. He is seized by a mood of inspiration and envisions the immortality of Lena and the earth: "*good stock peopling in tranquil obedience to it the good earth; from these hearty loins without hurry or haste descending mother and daughter*". His vision, it will be noted, is of the reproductive female carrying life forward with no limitation of time. When his experience is over, Hightower walks home through the woods. He experiences again the "savage fecundity of the earth", and he is lifted once more to a state of joy and communion:

[16]   *Ibid.*, p. 23.
[17]   *Ibid.*, p. 25.
[18]   *Ibid.*, p. 350.

"I must do this more often", he thinks, feeling the intermittent sun, the heat, smelling the savage and fecund odor of the earth, the woods, the loud silence. "I should never have lost this habit, too. But perhaps they will both come back to me, if this itself be not the same as prayer."

When he arrives home and goes to sleep his face is changed; it is now "innocent, peaceful, and assured".[19] For a moment at least he has been renewed by a creative force. Lena Grove has brought Hightower back to life; she has led him to a spiritual state he could never achieve within his inflexible religious design.

Light in August is the tragedy of a man victimized by inflexible religious design and the destructive female principle; however, the figure of Lena Grove opening and closing the novel also suggests a final affirmative note. The victimization of Joe is the tragedy of "poor man, poor mankind", but Lena's peculiar idea at one point that the child she bears is really his child suggests a symbolic union between them. Perhaps the point is that Lena's child is an enduring child of mankind compensating for Joe's death. Perhaps the full meaning of Lena's affirmation and her relation to the tragedy of Christmas may be found in the title of the novel. The expression "light in August" is a Southern colloquialism used when speaking of a woman who has given birth in that month. However, as Alfred Kazin points out, a symbolism of light and dark is also used throughout the novel.[20] Lena Grove is light in August; therefore, she is life and light giver; mankind does not end with the death of the Son of Man, Joe Christmas, for through Lena there is another life, another man, another chance.

Lena Grove is Faulkner's fullest picture of the earth mother, but she is not the only one; the unnamed woman in the "Old Man" section of *The Wild Palms* is another mother in whom the birth process is symbolic. In contrast to Charlotte Rittenmeyer this woman is "opposed to romantic love because she is faithful to one of the natural laws of the universe – childbirth – and she is able to communicate her belief emotionally to the Mississippi

[19]   *Ibid.*, pp. 355-56.
[20]   Alfred Kazin, "The Stillness of *Light in August*", in *Interpretations of American Literature*, ed. Charles Feidelson, Jr. and Paul Brodtkorb, Jr., pp. 349-68.

jailbird, at least for the length of the river journey, that responsibility is more important than escape".[21] Beside the symbolic significance of childbirth, there is the symbol of the river. "Old Man" is a designation used along the Mississippi for the river, so in a real sense Faulkner is giving us his version of *Life On the Mississippi*. Twain's idyllic, bucolic world is not recreated. Life, represented by the river and the woman, is nature in its "savage", "implacable", and particularly "oblivious" state. The flooded river is oblivious of the struggle of the woman and the convict to survive; they are seized by a prodigiously indifferent force which threatens to consume them. And, as Zink points out, the woman is gripped by "a parallel force every bit as powerful and inexorable as the great flood on which both she and the convict float helplessly".[22] The convict's reaction to the river and the woman (life) is the same; he feels victimized: "When he looked upon the swelling and unmanageable body before him it seemed to him that it was not the woman at all but rather a separate demanding threatening inert yet living mass of which both he and she were equally victims." [23] However, the woman's reaction matches that of the river; she is as oblivious of the river as it is of her. Her symbolic role in the story represents the enduring, surviving, and saving power of a woman who makes the threatening elements of life (nature) sustain and fulfill her. She is an excellent literary example of a philosophy voiced by the god-figure Stein in Conrad's *Lord Jim*:

A man that is born falls into a dream like a man who falls into the sea. If he tries to climb out into the air as inexperienced people endeavor to do he drowns . . . No! I tell you! The way is to the destructive element submit yourself, and with the exertions of your hands and feet in the water make the deep, deep sea keep you up.[24]

Just so the woman submits herself to the convict, the river, the process of birth, and her submission becomes her participation in and projection of life.

21 Malin, *William Faulkner*, p. 45.
22 Zink, "Faulkner's Garden", pp. 141-42.
23 *The Wild Palms*, p. 154.
24 Joseph Conrad, *Lord Jim* (New York, 1920), pp. 137-38.

The woman in "Old Man" is an embodied function; what happens in the story is related to the convict. He is in jail because he attempted a robbery to get some Woolworth jewelry for a sweetheart. Disillusioned with love and life, he feels secure in prison. It is a safe womb to him, and the chains that bind him to other prisoners are like "umbilical cords". When he is sent to rescue the woman, he is thrust out into violent life again. He must submit himself to the "destructive element"; he must make the river work for him, and he must deliver the child to save the pregnant woman. Responsible living is forced upon him, like Hightower, and his immunity is momentarily broken. For this reason he is in sharp contrast to Harry Wilbourne, "the fool of love", in *The Wild Palms* who wishes to "escape from the world". Slatoff observes that

In the first narrative, a man kills the woman he loves; in the second a man is forced to take responsibility for a woman he does not love. In the first, the relationship between the man and the woman is, above all, sexual; in the second, the man and the woman never have sexual relations. The first man, trained as a doctor and using surgical instruments, performs an abortion upon his beloved which results in her death. The second man, ignorant and untrained, using a tin can, helps the woman he does not love to deliver a child.[25]

And the convict fulfills all these obligations, despite a repugnance and threat of meaninglessness. First of all, the woman repels him because she appears as "one single inert monstrous sentient womb",[26] and secondly, when his whole experience is over he reflects:

And this is all. This is what severed me violently from all I ever knew and did not wish to leave and cast me upon a medium I was born to fear, to fetch up at last in a place I never saw before and where I do not even know where I am.[27]

However, he has overcome his repugnance and loss of meaning, for what nature and the woman ask of him requires an affirmative answer because they have become a part of his own survival.

[25] Slatoff, *Quest for Failure*, p. 207.
[26] *The Wild Palms*, p. 163.
[27] *Ibid.*, p. 231.

Therefore, he assumes responsibility, fulfills his obligations to the woman and his superiors, and never attempts to escape. Ironically, he is given an additional ten years in jail for being gone so long, and his final word (also the final word of the novel), "Women!" indicates he has not learned much or abated his repugnance. The point is, I believe, that the convict is moral without being aware of it in exactly the same way as the woman and the Old Man. His final word reflects an old adage about women that is the point of contrast in the two stories of *The Wild Palms:* you can't live with them and you can't live without them. Obviously the earth mother is one no man lives without.

As important as the earth mother is in Faulkner's fiction, her role is only preparatory to a second function of motherhood – the tender and loving care of the young. No earth mother is ever shown growing into this role; instead Faulkner illustrates the creative power of such responsible care through foster mothers. In Faulkner the colored mammy sometimes fills the void left by a natural mother who, like Mrs. Compson or Temple Drake in *Requiem for a Nun,* pursues private ends at the expense of her children. Faulkner's respect for the colored mammy is indicated in his dedication of *Go Down Moses.*

To Mammy

Caroline Barr
Mississippi
(1840–1940)

Who was born in slavery and who gave to my family a fidelity without stint or calculation of recompense and to my childhood an immeasurable devotion and love.[28]

"Fidelity" is one word that Faulkner uses frequently to characterize the foster mothers. They are true to their responsibilities even at a personal cost. Even so they possess other virtues as well. In "The Bear" Faulkner says that the Negroes are better than the whites because they have "pity and tolerance and forbear-

---

[28] It is hard to believe that Maxwell Geismar thinks that Faulkner has a "Great Hatred" for the female and the Negro when one considers this dedication.

ance and fidelity and love of children whether their own or not or
black or not".[29] There are no better words than these to describe
the full character and role of the colored foster mother. Furthermore, the mammy is always assumed to have the proper relationship to nature. (The Negroes are automatically associated with
the earth in Faulkner's mind because they have never been cut
off from it.) The faithful Negro servant graces almost every
"authentic" Southern romance from *Uncle Tom's Cabin* to *Gone
with the Wind*; however, in Faulkner's hands the colored mammy
is only used as a contrast in tragic circumstances. Whereas selfish
mothers bring defeat and destruction, she lives amid tragic forces
representing what Faulkner calls "female victory which is: endure and then endure without rhyme or reason or hope of reward
– and then endure".[30] Pity, tolerance, forbearance, and fidelity
all help the foster mother in her responsibility but again and again
her actions indicate that "love of children" is the key to her
endurance. She above all is willing to suffer that "little children
may come to Him unanguished, and unterrified".[31] This is the
secret of her character and her creative power. Nancy Manningoe
of *Requiem for a Nun* and Aunt Molly Beauchamp of *Go Down
Moses* are foster mothers of this type, but the prime example is
Dilsey in *The Sound and the Fury*.

In the introduction to *The Sound and the Fury* Faulkner gives
a thumbnail sketch of all the leading characters. For Dilsey he
merely says, "They endured". This enigmatic statement has
puzzled many readers, but the explanation, I believe, is in keeping
with Dilsey's character as a colored mammy. Dilsey is not just a
single person; she represents a whole race that has endured because, Faulkner points out, "they are tougher than we are", because they possess the virtues of pity, tolerance, forbearance,
fidelity, and love of children.[32] Dilsey is referred to in the plural
because she is anonymous as a single individual, and her anonymity is a vital selflessness enabling her to endure the deepest trage-

[29] *Go Down Moses*, p. 295.
[30] *Absalom, Absalom!*, p. 144.
[31] *Requiem for a Nun*, p. 163.
[32] *Go Down Moses*, p. 295.

dy. The only note of victory in the entire novel is provided by Dilsey's enduring love.

Dilsey's love continually puts her in stark contrast to every member of the Compson household. The history of the whole family is a tale told by an idiot full of sound and fury, but Dilsey's life is one of vision and serenity. She has seen "de first and de last" and "de power and de glory", because she loves the "Lamb of God that taketh away the sin of the world".[33] Quentin is as time-obsessed as Dilsey is timeless; he fights time to deny certain knowledge; Dilsey's love enables her to accept anything. Jason is a vicious exploiter; Dilsey a tender protector. Mr. Compson is an educated fool; Dilsey an uneducated seer. Caddy and Mrs. Compson are unfaithful mothers; Dilsey is a faithful mother *to* both of them and *for* both of them, even to the children they neglect. Long after the Compson family has destroyed itself, Dilsey endures, lives on, loves still.

Dilsey's actions in the novel show her to be warm-hearted, tireless, scolding, shrewd, and fearless. She has raised all the Compsons, feeding them, dressing them, cooking for them, protecting them. Her attitude toward Benjy and Quentin-the-girl best exemplifies the quality of care in her ministering love. Although Mrs. Compson regards her idiot son as a reproach and a punishment and wants to change his name, Dilsey accepts him along with all of the other children and opposes the change, feeling "he aint wore out the one he got yet".[34] Dilsey is willing to be associated with Benjy anywhere. When her own children chide her for bringing Benjy to church because people will talk, Dilsey says, "Den you send um to me, tell um de good Lawd dont keer whether he smart er not. Dont nobody but white trash keer dat." [35] Dilsey's favorite term of endearment for Ben is "honey", and her concern for him is just as tender and sweet. Her characteristic gesture is one of soothing care: "Dilsey stroked Ben's head slowly and steadily, smoothing the bang upon his brow." [36] Dilsey's treat-

---

[33] *The Sound and the Fury*, p. 313.
[34] *Ibid.*, p. 50.
[35] *Ibid.*, p. 306.
[36] *Ibid.*, p. 304.

ment of Caddy's illegitimate daughter Quentin reflects the same love and devotion. When the infant comes to live in the Compson house, Mrs. Compson is shocked and regards the child as another reproach upon her. Dilsey, however, feels the child belongs to her. " 'And whar else do she belong?' Dilsey says. 'Who else gwine raise her 'cep me? Aint I raised eve'y one of y'all?' " Dilsey puts the baby in her own room, and Mrs. Compson says " 'In there . . .? To be contaminated by that atmosphere? It'll be hard enough as it is, with the heritage she already has'." Dilsey's response is: "Why aint she gwine sleep in here? . . . In the same room whar I put her ma to bed ev'y night of her life since she was big enough to sleep by herself." [37] As Quentin grows, Dilsey protects her from Jason. When Jason wants to beat the little girl, Dilsey says, " 'Hit me den . . . if nothin else but hittin somebody wont do you. Hit me.' " Dilsey is sure of her power as well: " 'Now, now', she says, 'He aint gwine so much as lay his hand on you while Ise here'." [38] And as long as Dilsey is in the Compson household she carries on in the same way. Only when Jason finally dispossesses her is he able to send Benjy away to the state insane asylum. Faulkner was once asked if he would call the characters in *The Sound and the Fury* "good people". He answered: "I would call them tragic people. The good people, Dilsey, the Negro woman, she was a good human being. That she held that family together for not the hope of reward but just because it was the decent and proper thing to do." [39] Dilsey's treatment of Benjy and Quentin is typical of the decent and proper things she does – not for reward but for love.

A number of critics attach a great deal of significance to Dilsey's role in *The Sound and The Fury*, believing it is Dilsey who supplies an order and a moral perspective to the novel.[40] Others are not so certain of this.[41] However, all agree on the elements of

[37] *Ibid.*, p. 216.
[38] *Ibid.*, p. 203.
[39] Gwynn and Blotner, *Faulkner in the University*, p. 85.
[40] Mrs. Vickery in *The Novels of William Faulkner* and Peter Swiggart in "Moral and Temporal Order in *The Sound and the Fury*" follow this line of thought.
[41] Slatoff in his *Quest for Failure* is confused by Dilsey, and Malin in

her character and the quality of her love. Waggoner expresses my view by saying, "It may not be utterly fanciful to see her as becoming, finally, a kind of foster-mother of Christ [Benjy], the enabling agent of a revelation at once spiritual and aesthetic." [42] Dilsey's love is the total gift of a good woman; it provides the focus for her vision and is the means of her timeless transcendence. Her love is creative and renewing as long as it is received or valued. Her care of the Compsons is the figurative projection of the protective love of Christ in the novel. The rejection by the Compson children of such compassion and care is evidence of their tragic failure as people, for it symbolizes their rejection of order, love, and spiritual faith in all of life.

We turn now to the third mother figure in Faulkner's fiction — the granny — another mother surrogate who gives to youth an indispensable insight into the truth of life. In his discussion of Faulkner's women Malin classifies the women in this category as asexual and says:

Here we can find traditional images of the mother and the grandmother (or old spinster), both of whom have lost their active association with Eros. It is obvious that Faulkner has respect for these women, knowing they cannot use their beauty or repression to destroy men. This is not to say that they don't exhibit strong will power. All of his women do, but ... the will, although aggressive is humanitarian.[43]

This is a good summary of the qualities that characterize the grandmother — *agape*, aggressive willfulness, and humanitarian purposes. Her "proper sphere" is once again the immemorial earth suggested by her love and management of her garden, a place where she is continually found. The joy she receives from flowers and vegetables indicates her association with the chain of life. Her function is to be a guide and an instructor for youth. Beginning with Aunt Jenny Du Pre in *Sartoris*, Faulkner perfected the type with Rosa Millard in *The Unvanquished* and Miss Habersham in *Intruder in the Dust*. These characters are very reminiscent of Twain's Widow Douglas; all of them are crotchety

<hr>

William Faulkner and O'Connor in *Tangled Fire* scarcely mention Dilsey.
[42] Waggoner, *From Jefferson to the World*, p. 46.
[43] Malin, *William Faulkner*, p. 38.

and impatient, informed and purposeful, loving and loyal. Each of them is associated with boys for whom "Granny" is a moral conscience.

An understanding of Faulkner's view of child psychology is necessary in order to see when and why a youth needs a substitute moral conscience. In an interview recorded in *The Paris Review* for 1956 Faulkner was asked some direct questions about the nature of childhood. He explained that he felt

> The child has the capacity to do but it cannot know ... the will of the child gets stronger, more dangerous, but it has not begun to learn to know yet. Since his capacity to do is forced into channels of evil through environment and pressure, man is strong before he is moral.[44]

This statement explains the problem of a good many of Faulkner's sick heroes. The natural absence of knowledge in a youth leaves him susceptible to forces of destruction. In a sense, he is a victim of necessity operating through environment and pressure. Youths like Bayard Sartoris and Chick Mallison are given instructors in morality like Gavin Stevens or Miss Habersham in order that they may learn to know the truth of human character, human motives, and human needs. Faulkner's picture of youth, therefore, is the picture of a struggle to understand the mysterious knowledge of the human affair. When a youth is conjoined to a loving mother substitute, like a grandmother, we have a literary fusion as typical as the colored servant in the Southern household.

Faulkner's initial figure of this type, Aunt Jenny Du Pre, is an old woman with a biting tongue; she perpetuates the Sartoris legend, runs the Sartoris house, scolds the Negroes, and serves as a prophet of doom for Bayard Sartoris. She outlives all the foolish recklessness and violence of the Sartorises, alternately cussing them and loving them. Her chief characteristic is a prim and firm morality that is a perpetuation of the past glory of Southern womanhood. Although she is partially responsible for enlarging the Sartoris legend to the dimensions of a destructive myth, Miss Jenny deflates young Bayard's actions and the whole tradition.

[44] Interview in *The Paris Review*, Spring, 1956, reprinted in Malcolm Cowley, ed., *Writers at Work: The Paris Review Interviews* (New York, Viking Press, 1958), pp. 122-141; p. 131.

Mrs. Vickery notes that, "Her willingness to criticize as well as admire and to modify as well as preserve reveals a flexibility lacking in the male Sartorises." [45] She would have whipped Bayard for his wildness, for she senses his headlong rush to doom. "This Cassandra-like strain is important; it indicates both her shrewdness and strict moral standard." [46] Bayard ignores the truth available from this old woman, causing Miss Jenny to lament of his "humorless and fustian vain-glory".[47] After Bayard's death Aunt Jenny attempts to be a help to his wife and son. She is shocked to discover that her daughter-in-law has slept with a blackmailer in order to retrieve some erotic letters. Her death, like the incident of the letters, is conveyed in a short story entitled "There Was a Queen", a title indicative of Faulkner's high regard of her.

Another "granny" that Faulkner regards with something like awe is Rosa Millard of *The Unvanquished*. She is a highly romanticized figure who leads a guerrilla movement against the invading Northern Armies. Most of her actions suggest a firm moral standard and an aggressive willfulness. She hides her grandson and his colored playmate under her skirts when the Union troops are searching for them; she helps rebuild her neighbor's ruined farms; she steals mules from the Union Army, then sells them back; and she runs the local church single-handed. However, she keeps accounts of all her spoils of war, for she is a religious person and knows that one day the books will be settled. Granny is somewhat troubled about her relationship to God, for she has been cussing, stealing, and fighting; however, she says, "I sinned for justice" [48] and leaves it at that. By her side in all of her actions is young Bayard Sartoris (*old* Bayard Sartoris in the Faulkner legend) and Ringo, his Negro friend. They form the principal audience for Granny's actions. Granny's active participation in a worthy cause and her prim morality are inspirational to the boys, a fact enforced by the intensity with which they avenge her murder. Rosa Millard is a picture of the Southern woman whom the war

[45] Vickery, *The Novels of William Faulkner*, p. 25.
[46] Malin, *William Faulkner*, p. 39.
[47] *Sartoris*, p. 374.
[48] *The Unvanquished*, p. 94.

"emancipated", but it would almost appear that Faulkner feels the only time it is safe for a woman to assert her individuality is when her function as child bearer has ceased. Only then can she, as Rosa Millard illustrates, rise "to actual stardom in the role of matriarch, arbitrating from the fireside corner of a crone the pride and destiny of her family".[49]

The only grandmother figure that Faulkner develops with real depth is the kinless Miss Habersham of *Intruder in the Dust*. The entire movement of this novel is a series of actions that Miss Habersham and young Chick Mallison undertake together despite the disapprobation and rigid mores of an inflexible community. The joint involvement of this "grandmother" and the youth demonstrates her willingness to act upon instinct and principle and his willingness to follow and learn. Chick Mallison feels compelled to help a Negro accused of murder, Lucas Beauchamp. This compulsion goes against all Chick's tradition and training. Miss Habersham supports and joins him in this venture because she has known Lucas and his wife Molly all of her life. (Molly was born the same time as she seventy years ago.) She refuses to recognize the crime as a Negro act. She inspires and actually helps Chick and Aleck Saunders dig up the corpse of the victim to prove its identity. Later she stands guard in the prison to prevent any possible lynching of Lucas because the sheriff knows a mob would respect her. The sheriff and Gavin Stevens, the attorney, are dumbfounded that Miss Habersham, "whose name was now the oldest which remained in the county", and who was "a kinless spinster of seventy living in the columned colonial house on the edge of town", would join in digging up a grave to prove a Negro innocent of a crime. Stevens keeps repeating, "She's too old for this" but corrects it to "No a woman a lady shouldn't have to do this".[50] But Miss Habersham does it because she knows that men are restricted by tradition, for she explains:

Lucas knew it would take a child or an old woman like me: someone not concerned with probability, with evidence. Men like your uncle

---

[49] *Absalom, Absalom!*, p. 69.
[50] *Intruder in the Dust*, p. 112.

and Mr. Hampton [the sheriff] have had to be men too long, busy too long.[51]

Miss Habersham discerns truth without the inhibitions of the male and by her actions confirms the insights of a matriarch who is willing to cross mores in order to reveal the truth. And her willingness to become engaged has an inspiring effect on Chick:

... but it was only after Miss Habersham came around the house and spoke to him that he knew he was going to go through with it and he remembered again what old Ephraim had told him after they found the ring under the hog trough: *If you got something outside the common run that's got to be done and cant wait, dont waste your time on the menfolks; they works on what your uncle calls the rules and the cases. Get the womens and the children at it; they works on the circumstances.*[52]

Miss Habersham acts in spite of rules and cases, and Chick learns because he is willing to follow her. She possesses the ability to reduce abstract truth to simple reality. When she explains some involved problem to Chick, he sees

what Miss Habersham paraphrased was simple truth, not even fact and so there was not needed a great deal of diversification and originality to express it because truth was universal, it had to be universal to be truth and so there didn't need to be a great deal of it just to keep running something no bigger than one earth and so anybody could know truth; all they had to do was just to pause, just to stop, just to wait.[53]

Chick has learned something about the nature of truth itself; he senses its character and feels he is aware of a method of attaining it. In other words, he has gained some kind of moral awareness through this spinster "grandmother". Her educative function toward Chick has led Malin to observe that Faulkner has made her "a symbol of what he praises in Man: the potentiality to respect and save himself without the artificiality of ritual. And she is reflected in Faulkner's image of the mother."[54]

[51] *Ibid.*, pp. 89, 90.
[52] *Ibid.*, p. 112.
[53] *Ibid.*, p. 89.
[54] Malin, *William Faulkner*, p. 60.

When all of the various mother substitutes in Faulkner's fiction are considered, it is interesting to note that no one of them is ever developed with a man or as a part of a family; the earth mother is pregnant but not married; the foster mother may have a husband, but he is not a part of the action; the grandmother is either a widow or a spinster. The surrogate mother loves in a family situation that offers no apparent reward. In a family situation characterized by a father promoting social designs and women who are irresponsible and self-centered, it is the surrogate mother who offers a filial love that is spiritual in nature.

For Faulkner mother love is "the more excellent way" of St. Paul, for mother love is enduring, a love that will "suffer" birth, idiocy, perversion, sin, failure, and ignorance. Besides being long-suffering, this love is compassionate and gentle – we see Dilsey stroking Ben's head, Lena Grove suckling her baby, Rosa Millard tenderly tucking Bayard and Ringo into bed. And it is also comprehending love – Dilsey really knows very little but she has seen all, the beginning and the end, the power and the glory, and Miss Habersham discerns the reality hidden behind the facade of tradition, ritual and social respectability.

As we have observed the fragmented parts of mother love depicted in Faulkner's novels, we also see that the mother surrogates are figures of isolated strength. They live beyond the influences that mold men and women into conformists. They have no compulsion to express their individuality; therefore, they are content to live unto themselves and their functions in life. Since they are in isolation, they feel no threat or power of a design; consequently, they are no respecters of persons, black or white, dead or alive. They have a joy in life that they gain from a separation unto the earth and young, uncorrupted life. When considered as a whole, they are seen to be loving, strong, joyful women willing to act on behalf of others.

The only creative love Faulkner pictures in the female is mother love; romantic love is the subject of his tragic novels. There death and love are one, for there sex is misunderstood to be love or sought in its place. Faulkner dramatizes this as one of the basic errors of our age and one of the causes of our tragic experiences. "Female victory" and "the destructive female principle", therefore, is Faulkner's way of picturing love and death in the female. Although the greater part of his fiction suggests that the tragic power of a woman is common and typical, it must be noted that he does conceive of a "good" woman. Mother love is certainly not the answer to the problem of love between the sexes; nor does Faulkner intend it to be. He offers us no answer. But since he centers so much of his fiction on childhood, adolescence, and young adulthood, it is certain that in these stages of life mother love is a sustaining and creative force.

SOCIETY

V. SNOPESISM

Q.: This callous attitude of Sutpen and Flem Snopes, the ability to use people without realizing they're people, sort of dehumanizing them, it seems to gradually get worse as they go from country into town and cities. Is that a definite, is that a conscious thing?

A.: It didn't get worse because they came into cities. They had to come into cities to find more people to use. But it got worse because of the contempt which the ability to use people develops in anyone. There are very few people that have enough grandeur of soul to be able to use people and not develop contempt for them. And that – the contempt for people came not because they moved to the city but out of success.

Faulkner in the University

The character of modern man, and some of his behavior, is partially explained by the structure of modern society and his position in it. At least an increasing number of social philosophers seem to be saying this. For instance, Louis Wirth feels that the urban influence in modern life has caused the abstract characteristics of "size", "density", and "heterogeneity" to result in "the substitution of secondary for primary contacts, the weakening of the bonds of kinship plus the declining social significance of the family, the disappearance of the neighborhood, and the undermining of the traditional bases of social solidarity".[1] A society with these characteristics leads some social analysts to think man is at the mercy of his social structure. To illustrate, Karl Jaspers says modern man is a prey to technical dominance and consequently is bereft of his world. The technical life order

[1] Louis Wirth, "Urbanism as a Way of Life", *Reader in Urban Sociology*, ed. Paul K. Hatt and Albert J. Reiss, Jr. (Illinois, 1951), pp. 32-49.

eventually ousts man himself. "Cast adrift in this way", says Jaspers, "lacking all sense of historical continuity with past or future, man cannot remain man." [2] Wirth and Jaspers fear the urban and economic base of modern society because it seems to divorce man from responsible living in terms of love and compassion. Erich Fromm in *Escape from Freedom* describes the economic warfare that can eclipse a personal relationship in society.

What Protestantism had started to do in freeing man spiritually, capitalism continued to do mentally, socially, and politically. Economic freedom was the basis of this development, the middle class was its champion. The individual was no longer bound by a fixed social system, based on tradition with a comparatively small margin for personal advancement beyond the traditional limits. He was allowed and expected to succeed in personal economic gains as far as his diligence, intelligence, courage, thrift, or luck would lead him. His was the chance of success, his was the risk to lose and to be one of those killed or wounded in the fierce economic battle in which each one fought against everybody else.[3]

In general these social philosophers feel the technical evolution of modern life creates abstract – that is to say unreal or non-spiritual values. The emphasis on material gain, they feel, weakens man's blood ties and diminishes his concern for others. Modern man, therefore, is thought to be in search of a soul, because he has lost touch with his spiritual nature in the midst of a materialistic society where his way of thought is too strongly influenced by the urban and capitalistic mentality. Modern man in this state is a potentially destructive force.

It is the destructive force in modern man that Faulkner writes of as he discusses Popeye in *Sanctuary*, Harry Wilbourne in *The Wild Palms* and the Snopeses in *Snopes*. These men are creatures of the modern American age, and they project the values of the age through their nature and their uses of power.

Contemporary American man, as Faulkner sees him, is threatened by a lack of compassion – Jung's soullessness. Instead of the concern and kinship that should typify human relations, men

---

[2] Karl Jaspers, *Man in the Modern Age* (New York, 1957), p. 42.
[3] Fromm, *Escape from Freedom*, p. 106.

lose their human response within an inhuman economic standard which society now accepts conventionally. This lack of compassion plus the tactics of opportunism, typical of our age, is reflected in human beings beyond compassion and morality – human beings who prey upon other people, using them as tools to gain money. Flem Snopes is the particular creation of Faulkner to represent this incarnation of predatory amorality; in Flem's actions we read the destructive record of man's inhumanity to man under the cloak of respectability for the express purpose of material reward. Faulkner exhibits an intense dislike for men like Flem, for to his mind they violate the verities of the heart that distinguish man – the chief of which is the capacity to endure through love.

Faulkner joins company with D. H. Lawrence at this point, for in his early and late period Lawrence felt the same wrath for the abstract ideals of a materialistic and loveless society. In *Lady Chatterley's Lover* Lawrence tried to express through the figure of Clifford the viciousness and impotency of men and societies who have deserted blood and the flesh for material gains and a selfish, isolated existence. There is an interesting parallel between Clifford and Flem Snopes. Each represents the false gods of his society. Clifford's position of authority over the miners who work for him is like Flem's control over the people who owe him money. Flem and Clifford are married to women of unusual sexual potency or potential, yet these men are impotent which suggests they have cold natures and lack vital creativity. Despite the fact that Flem and Clifford are cuckolded, the balance of power in their society falls to them because weak people and social convention empower them to flout and defeat the traditional responsibilities of kinship and love. Flem and Clifford are modern men without souls and they represent the type of behavior that undermines the traditional bases of social solidarity.

Faulkner always shows a relationship between the inhuman man and his society. He is outraged at man's inhumanity, his lack of love, his tightly designed life, the tragic destruction he forces upon others. But he can never let him go without showing him as the product of society itself. In the case of Thomas Sutpen, Faulkner tries to indicate that his inhuman inflexibility results from the inhuman design of Southern society in general. Popeye's inhuman treatment of people and animals is shown to be the outgrowth of his inheritance and his environment. Flem Snopes's soulless treatment of people is an outcome of the depersonalized nature of finance capitalism. Men like Sutpen, Popeye, and Flem are culprits without doubt, but their inhumanity is activated by a society that can produce, tolerate, or even approve of them.

Eventually Flem Snopes becomes the dominant symbol of predatory amorality in Faulkner's fiction; however, in *Sanctuary* Faulkner attempts to express the relationship between an amoral individual and his society in the figure of Popeye. Malcolm Cowley sees Popeye's inhuman acts "as a social symbol. It is somehow connected in the author's mind with the rape of the South." [14] In Faulkner's view the rape of the South was accomplished in part by a Northern society depersonalized by mechanization. Thus Popeye is shown to be the product of a mechanical age, and through images Faulkner attempts to suggest a relationship between Popeye's inhumanity and the depersonalized nature of his society. Popeye is most frequently described in mechanical terms; his general appearance possesses that "vicious depthless quality of stamped tin", his eyes look "like rubber knobs", and "his face just went away, like the face of a wax doll set too near a hot fire and forgotten". His tight suit and stiff hat are "all angles, like a modernistic lampshade". Faulkner says that men like Popeye have "a hard ruthless quality, not immoral but unmoral". He indicates that the dehumanized criminal like Popeye is, "so single, so hard and ruthless, so impeccable in amorality, as to have a kind of integrity, purity, who would not only never need nor intend to forgive anyone anything, he would never even realize that anyone expected him to forgive anyone anything". [5] This "impeccable amorality" is the difference between moral and immoral and is a precise description of the society in which Popeye is raised – a society characterized by indifference reflected

[4] William Faulkner, *The Portable Faulkner*, ed. Malcolm Cowley (New York, 1946), p. xiii.
[5] *Requiem for a Nun*, p. 171.

in the total absence of morality. Popeye's father is a professional
strike breaker from whom he inherits syphilis which weakens his
body as well as his mind. He has a pyromaniac for a grandmother.
Five years of his early life are spent in reform school. By supplying these details of Popeye's heredity and environment, Faulkner
suggests that these influences make Popeye the inhuman person
he is. He attempts, in the next to last section of *Sanctuary,* to
indicate that Popeye's inhumanity and brutality reflect his background as well as his character. Faulkner's early concern to account for the evil in amoral characters reveals his desire to relate
personal evil to the nature of social force itself.

Furthermore, Faulkner sees that social force can create an un-
challenged social conformity that can destroy individual compassion and character. In *The Wild Palms*, Faulkner makes a detailed
analysis of the dangers in social conformity. Through the figure
of Harry Wilbourne, a man struggling to experience life and love,
Faulkner attempts to show that the power of conformity in society
creates a desire for social "respectability". He indicates that
"respectability" not only restricts men in the search for self, it
can also be used as a tool by others to gain power and wealth.
The homage to respectability can be destructive in more ways
than one.

In *The Wild Palms* Harry is a social outcast because of his love
affair. The social pressure he feels leads him to consider what it is
that causes people to value respectability. "I have clearly seen,
followed out the logical conclusion, that it is one of what we call
the prime virtues – thrift, industry, independence – that breeds
all the vices – fanaticism, smugness, meddling, fear, and worst of
all respectability." [6] To Harry respectability is the worst vice because it is hypocritical – it uses signs of grace as a pretext of
inner purity. Harry is defying social convention by his illicit love
affair, attempting thereby to come to a greater sense of self-
realization. He senses that the desire for respectability crushes the
self by its hypocrisy and leads people to make their lives conform
to a social norm. As Harry points out, "it's not avocation that
elects our vocations, it's respectability that makes chiropractors

[6] *The Wild Palms*, p. 133.

and clerks and bill posters and motormen and pulp writers out of us".[7] The desire for respectability eliminated Christ from society, Harry thinks, and respectability even threatens to do away with love. Harry fights the social conformity that is implied by the pressures of social convention:

They [society] had used respectability on me and that was harder to beat than money. So I am vulnerable in neither money or respectability now and so They will have to find something else to force upon us to conform to the pattern of human life which has now evolved to do without love – to conform or die.[8]

By attempting to live for love, by actually being the fool of love, Harry enters a protest against the loveless and amoral nature of society.

These two characteristics then, a socially induced amorality and the use of respectability as a tool, display the sickness of society itself to Faulkner, and throughout the Snopes trilogy he attempts to illustrate the point that a predatory amorality operates under the cloak of respectability. The individual and society are equally guilty, as the machinations of Flem Snopes in the village, the town, and the mansion reveal. *The Hamlet* pictures Flem as an inhuman economic exploiter; in *The Town* Flem is seen in anxious pursuit of all of the badges of respectability; in *The Mansion* Flem uses his respectability to gain his own favorite end – money. Warren Beck in his full-length study of the Snopes trilogy asks this question about Flem Snopes: "Is not this amoral creature a more specifically modern kind of villain, the ethical nihilist?"[9] The answer to this question is an unqualified yes. The progression of Flem's character is a study of the economic growth of modern man and the intrinsic relation he bears to the society that forms him. The destruction that Flem Snopes imposes really results from the meddling, smugness, fanaticism, fear, lust, and greed that characterize a society that is merely respectable. Faulkner's study of the destructive force of amorality in the Snopes

---

[7]   *Ibid.*, p. 133.
[8]   *Ibid.*, p. 140.
[9]   Warren Beck, *Man in Motion: Faulkner's Trilogy* (Madison, 1961), p. 88.

trilogy is a picture of society being devoured by its young. And
in this picture, as Beck notes,

> Flem seems the ultimate of the amoral, so much so that he can hardly
> be accounted cruel, being merely insensitive, literally ruthless. It is
> thereby that he becomes a pivotal point in the trilogy's structure and
> theme.[10]

In order to get a clear picture of Flem as the all-embracing image
of destructive amorality it is necessary to trace his actions through
all three volumes. This process will reveal the growth of Flem's
power, his total lack of soul and compassion, his inhuman economic standard of values, and the ruin he brings to others.

The Hamlet is a book structured in a series of intricate contrasts. The main contrast is between the non-aristocratic world
of Frenchman's Bend, emotional and genuine, and the rational
and materialistic world of the Snopeses recognized by Ratliff, the
characteristic Faulknerian commentator, as the enemy.[11] Although
the novel is composed of various stories, they all refer, finally, to
Flem; the various contrasts are patterned about the conflict between the two worlds. T. Y. Greet discerns that "the development of the novel is governed by the significant contrasts between
rationally and emotionally motivated action".[12] Flem represents
an inhuman and an amoral rationalism, and when the patterned
contrasts of the stories unfold, Flem – or one of the Snopeses –
is revealed as the rational manipulator of human emotion aimed
at effecting a private gain.

In the way he disposes of Jody Varner, in his rise to power in
Frenchmen's Bend, in gulling the natives with wild horses, and
in his duping of Ratliff, Flem shows himself to be beyond appetite,
pride, passion, and fidelity. Faulkner, therefore, chooses to characterize Flem and his family by images suggesting animal greed
and amorality. Flem has the "predatory nose of a hawk"; he is
"froglike" and he is compared to a spider. I. O. Snopes is likened

to a weasel and St. Elmo Snopes to a goat. Miss Viola Hopkins
has noted that Faulkner's repeated association of Flem with animals suggests that rather than being in harmony with the natural
world, Flem and his family are presented as a sub-human species
who merge with the lower orders.[13] Flem is a fox, possessing an
impenetrable craftiness and a genius for manipulation that is aug-
mented by an imaginative cunning. And Faulkner illustrates
Flem's characteristics in two ways: first, Flem is discovered as
the cause of most of the events in the story; secondly, his amoral
nature is continually developed by a constant refinement of images. Faulkner culminates his development of Flem's character
with the assertion that Flem is soulless. Despite the fact that the
story of Flem's descent to hell is a mock epic, the humor must not
obscure what Faulkner is saying about him.

No one narrates the story of Flem's descent: the account is
merely an italicized insertion, best understood as an editorial
comment. Flem shows up in hell to claim his soul which he de-
posited there in order to gain power on earth. When his soul cannot be located, Flem approaches the Prince of Hell:

'Well.' the prince says.
He turned his head and spit, the spit frying off the floor quick in
a little blue ball of smoke. 'I come about that soul', he says.
'So they tell me', the Prince says. 'But you have no soul.'
'Is that my fault?' he says.
'Is it mine?' the Prince says. 'Do you think I created you?'
'Then who did'? he says. And he had the Prince there and the
Prince knowed it.[14]

As the account ends the Prince of Hell is deposed from his throne,
for he recognizes in Flem his superior. In a comic way Faulkner
is making his most telling point — there is not one human thing
about Flem, not even the nature that resides beneath his inhuman
acts. The devil has no power over Flem, for he possesses no bargaining position. Flem has nothing to lose. Flem would never fit
into Sartre's hell which is "other people", for he never relates to
others. It is easy to see, therefore, that Flem is not a figure to be

[13]   Viola Hopkins, "William Faulkner's *The Hamlet:* A Study in Meaning
and Form", *Accent*, XV (Spring, 1955), p. 138.
[11]   *The Hamlet*, pp. 153-54.

understood existentially. The key to his character is to see him as a projection of a depersonalized social system. Flem's rise to power in the hamlet is the unfolding of his inhumane and amoral destructive power, and this can best be demonstrated by examining each of the four books of *The Hamlet* in detail.

Faulkner divides *The Hamlet* into four sections. The first section, called simply "Flem", is the narrative account of Flem's rise to power in Frenchman's Bend. Starting out as a sharecropper, Flem parlays the threat of a possible barn burning into a position in the Varner store. Through several business deals, Flem skins the local citizens and begins to implant his relatives about the entire village. Old Man Varner, who practically controls all of Frenchman's Bend, exhibits a grudging respect for Flem, and eventually Flem replaces Varner's son, Jody, as Varner's prime minister. The village and Ratliff are held in awe, but only Ratliff seems to sense the destruction that is latent in the Snopeses' rise to power. At the end of the first section Flem is seen enthroned upon Old Man Varner's special chair of authority, a position achieved through threatened destruction, manipulation, and a hard-headed unconcern for anything but profit.

Section two is Eula's story, and the contrast here is between her two emotional love affairs and her eventual loveless marriage to Flem. Even though she is worshipped by the school teacher, La Bove, and violently conquered by the dashing Hoake McCarron, Eula – pregnant – is finally settled on Flem as a part of a "business" deal. Eula symbolizes all the power and beauty of feminine fecundity; consequently, the school teacher speculates that her husband would have to be

a dwarf, a gnome, without glands or desire, who would be no more a physical factor in her life than the owner's name on the fly-leaf of a book ... the crippled Vulcan to that Venus, who would not possess her but merely own her ... as he might own ... a field say. He saw it: the fine land rich and fecund and foul and eternal and impervious to him who claimed title to it, oblivious, drawing to itself tenfold the quantity of living seed its owner's whole life could have secreted and compounded, producing a thousandfold the harvest he could ever hope to gather and save.[15]

[15] *Ibid.*, p. 119.

Throughout the novel the productive or fecund female is associated with the land in this manner – Houston makes the same
association with Lucy, his wife, and I. O. Snopes does the same
with his love, the cow. Eula's marriage to Flem is a sacrifice of
the earth goddess to the unbeliever, and the symbolism is aug-
mented by the decline of the crops in Frenchman's Bend. T. Y.
Greet says, "This is the crux of the novel, that the favor of the
gods – Love, Fertility – has been sacrificed to rational opportunism." [16] There is more to it than this, however; the rich land
has been offered in sacrifice by a village representative, the high
priest, Old Man Varner. It is therefore apparent that rational
opportunism has infected the people, and the source of the infection is Flem Snopes.

The third section of the novel contains the love stories of Houston and Lucy and Ike Snopes and his cow. The contrast between
the love affairs is obvious, and both end on a tragic note. Lucy is
killed by Houston's stallion, and Ratliff forces Lump Snopes to
get rid of Ike's cow. Lump does what he is forced to do, but, in
contrast, Ratliff acts out of his humanity. Throughout the novel,
Ratliff is the emblem of the humane, ethical tradition. One further
point needs to be made about Ike's love for the cow. Faulkner
envelops this story with a lush, purple prose; this contrast between the style of the writing and the meaning of the action is
meant to underscore an important point: the nature of an amoral
society sometimes forces it to judge a "pure" love perverted; at
the same time it accepts a "perverted" love affair, like Flem and
Eula's, simply because all the norms of social convention have
been fulfilled.

The spotted horses episode dominates the fourth and last book
of *The Hamlet*. As far back as *Sartoris* Faulkner had used the
horse as a symbol of destruction, and he repeats the use of the
symbol in this book. In the earlier portions of the book the horse
stories of Houston and Ab Snopes are individualized accounts of
destruction; the spotted horse episode involves the entire village.
All the citizens feel afraid of the wild horses, but a smooth-talking
salesman employed by Flem whets the desire of the men to pos-

[16]   Greet, "Theme and Structure in *The Hamlet*", p. 781.

sess the beasts, so that they pay their hard-earned money for un-
tamed animals that run wild. Russell Roth notes that the men of
the village "let their natural energies be manipulated by the same
emissary of evil [Flem] for purely monetary (that is to say, vi-
ciously abstract) and ultimately amoral ends".[17] The story of the
spotted horses, then, acts as a catalyst and serves to clarify two
aspects of the theme of the novel: the destructive nature of the
purely acquisitive instincts, and the susceptibility of acquisitive
man to rational manipulation. Flem is becoming more powerful
and successful because he is using his knowledge of men and society to effect greater schemes to gain money. This power and
success is illustrated again in the fourth book of *The Hamlet*
through the story of Flem's buried treasure, a story which again
demonstrates the destructive power of amoral behavior.

Flem salts a treasure field in order to dupe three men: Ratliff,
Henry Armstid, whom Flem has already partially ruined by allowing him to purchase a wild horse with his food money, and
Bookwright. Each of these men responds to the prospect of buried
treasure because of opportunism, but the destruction of Armstid
is out of proportion to his involvement. Armstid is so enraged at
finding no treasure that he refuses to accept the fact. His willing
suspension of disbelief becomes sheer madness, for he refuses to
accept the reality of the situation. He stays in the field frantically
searching for gold. As Flem leaves the village headed for the
town, he rides past the field where Armstid, days later, is still
digging for non-existent pirate treasure. Flem watches him chase
away some teasing boys, then

He came straight back to the trench, hurrying back to it with that
painful and laboring slowness, the gaunt unshaven face which was now
completely that of a madman. He got back into the ditch and began
to dig.
Snopes turned his head and spat over the wagon wheel. He jerked
the reins slightly. "Come up", he said.[18]

Flem feels no compassion for Armstid because the relationship

[17] Russell Roth, "The Centaur and the Pear Tree", *Western Review*,
XVI (Spring, 1952), p. 205.
[18] *The Hamlet*, p. 373.

between them is purely business. Armstid is a factor in an economic equation; Flem can be indifferent to him because he can be indifferent to himself. He has no compassion or feeling because economics has none. Flem leaves Armstid and the village for the town and a wider field of operation.

The Hamlet is the tragi-comic allegory of the corruption of a people. Frenchman's Bend is unable to deal with Flem because it has a double standard of values. All of the people want the same things as Flem, but they do not have the power of Flem's amorality. They are bound by their own limited notion of respectability even while they admire Flem for his shrewdness, his efficiency, and above all for his success. Flem uses the norms of social convention and their moral intent for his own purposes – that is, he makes the morality of others pay him. Hyatt Waggoner calls Flem's amoral economics the wedding of avarice and pure animality.

Flem is a destructive force in the village because he breaks up families, provokes men to madness, and redistributes the wealth and power in his favor. He preys upon the villagers with easy-term loans and foreclosed mortgages; he begins to use people as hostages, even manipulating the members of his own family to his private advantage. Flem is an impregnable destructive force because he possesses no emotional ties that can weaken him or bring to him the truths of the human heart – pity, love, courage, honor, and justice.

In the seventeen years between *The Hamlet* and *The Town* Faulkner added a great deal to his ideas of a destructive amorality produced by an acquisitive and rationalistic society. The difference between life in the hamlet and the town is the formalization of a corrupt standard that was only implicit in the backwoods country. The town, as Faulkner sees it, is an agglomeration of individuals who have grudgingly given up their individualism for a group conformity. The desire for "respectability" is a tyrannous force that compels people into patterns of behavior. In *The Town* Charles Mallison describes this condition:

ours a town established and decreed by people neither Catholics nor Protestants nor even atheists but incorrigible nonconformists, nonconformists not just to everybody else but to each other in mutual accord; a nonconformism defended and preserved by descendants whose ancestors hadn't quitted home and a security for a wilderness in which to find freedom of thought as they claimed and oh yes, believed, but to find freedom in which to be incorrigible and unreconstructible Baptists and Methodists; not to escape from tyranny as they claimed and believed, but to establish one.[19]

This is the kind of environment that encourages and admires the unscrupulous actions of Flem Snopes. As Steven Marcus points out: "It is utterly appropriate that a Snopes should come to power in this culture . . . he is the fulfillment of a tradition, its natural, purified, stripped-down product." [20]

When Flem reaches the town he pursues his design to achieve power and respectability. In time Flem's relatives infiltrate the town through his influence; however, their shady behavior begins to imperil Flem's facade of respectability and Flem will not stand for this because now, as Mrs. Littlejohn observes in *The Hamlet,* "the Snopes name . . . That's got to be pure as marble." First Flem rids the town of the dirty postcard show sponsored by Montgomery Ward Snopes, then he gets rid of the wild "Indian" children of another relative. Through actions like these Flem characterizes himself as the defender of "civic jealousy and pride". In reality he is protecting his respectability, for it is the key to his gaining wealth and power in the town.

Flem's ambition now includes the presidency of the bank, and he manipulates the members of his own family in order to gain the post. He is already a deacon in the Baptist church; if he gains control of the bank his public figure will be supported by the two strongest communal institutions – the church and the bank. In order to gain this position he uses the love affair between his wife and Manfred de Spain, the incumbent bank president. De Spain and Eula have come together in a "simple unadulterated uninhibited immortal lust", and their affair has been going on for years – eighteen of them. Flem threatens to tell his step-daughter, Linda, of the affair, and to prevent this, Eula and de Spain fall

---

[19] *The Town*, p. 307.
[20] Steven Marcus, "Snopes Revisited", *The Partisan Review*, XXIV, 3 (Summer, 1957), p. 440.

into his control. This, of course, eventually leads to their destruction. The whole town knows about Eula and de Spain and how
Flem is using them; admiration for Flem's cunning and unfeeling
behavior is boundless. Social pressure is on Flem's side, despite
the fact that he is using people as hostages. Jefferson indicts itself by its approval of Flem. Stevens, the county attorney, is almost at a point of despair over the latest victory of amoral power.
"Let us then give, relinquish Jefferson to the Snopeses, banker,
mayor, alderman, church and all, so that, in defending themselves
from Snopeses, Snopeses must of necessity defend and shield us,
their vassals and chattels." [21]

Eula is driven to suicide and de Spain is forced to flee in order
to protect her daughter. Eula panics because Flem tells her father
about the secret love affair, and old Man Varner comes in from
Frenchman's Bend to put an end to the threatened scandal. Old
Man Varner could not care less about his daughter's love affair,
but he fears Flem will make good his threat to make it public. In
order to control the affair and get rid of de Spain, Varner shifts
his bank stock to Flem, giving Flem control of the bank. Eula's
death is not an occasion of sorrow for Flem; he merely uses it as
another opportunity to enhance his respectability. He orders a
beautiful monument to be made for Eula. On it Flem has etched:
"A Virtuous Wife is a Crown to Her Husband. Her Children
Shall Rise Up and Call Her Blessed." Flem has actually destroyed
his wife in order to gain more respectability, more money, and
more power. Even the town must accept the ironic inscription on
the monument or reveal its own hypocrisy in tacitly approving
for eighteen years an adulterous affair. In *The Town* Flem
achieves the pinnacle of respectability: he is president of the
bank, a church deacon, a grieving widower, and a loving father.
But his own destruction is imminent and is recorded in the third
and last volume of the trilogy – *The Mansion*.

The Mansion shifts the focus from the destructive effect of a
predatory amorality to the destruction of amoral force itself. This
shift of focus is an index of Faulkner's concentration upon a new
force in the world, a force operating in man on behalf of humani-

[21] *The Town*, p. 44.

ty. Flem Snopes, the inhuman and coldly rational manipulator, is slain by Mink Snopes, a representative of the anonymous folk of the earth. Mink Snopes had been deserted by Flem during his trial for the murder of Houston. Mink's many years in jail have meta-morphosed him into an agent of retributive justice. Significantly, Mink represents not society but humanity. Society is Flem's ally; humanity is his victim and his enemy. The manner of Flem's death points up the fact that the conflict in *The Mansion* is no longer between Ratliff and the Snopeses or Gavin Stevens and the Snopeses. As Miss Kerr correctly states, "The chief action is no longer love and barter. What defeats Snopesism is Snopes itself; animal cunning and shrewdness without knowledge or imagina-tion." [22] An amoral cupidity is turned at last upon itself, for Flem is destroyed as a result of one of his own inhuman acts, fulfilling a prophecy Faulkner made before he published *The Mansion*: "The Snopeses will destroy themselves." [23]

Snopes, the trilogy, is Flem's story picturing a career of chi-canery and exploitation of the land and of man. He is like Dante's usurers; he does not till the land, and he makes no positive con-tribution to mankind through a creative skill. Flem is the full American embodiment of all the evil Ezra Pound sees in the modern U-S-U-R-E-R. Flem's manipulation of men's souls through their pocketbooks and his unearned wealth accumulated through "lawful" interest effectively characterize all the evil that Pound foresaw in a society that measures man by wealth rather than by worth. Pound, as a native of Idaho, would probably recog-nize Flem immediately. He would see Flem as a full flowering of every anti-Jeffersonian virtue, a throwback to the animal instincts that always imperil an enlightened aristocracy based on personal and nationalistic worth. As a matter of fact, the Snopeses as a whole represent a direct animal response to the values of money and power which control society. Of all the Snopeses, Flem has made the perfect adjustment; he sees how much of Snopes is hidden in everyone, in the men who possess money and the men who do not,

[22] Elizabeth M. Kerr, "Snopes", *Wisconsin Studies in Contemporary Literature*, 1, 2 (Spring-Summer, 1959), p. 75.
[23] Gwynn and Blotner, *Faulkner in the University*, p. 282.

and it is upon their secret charge of resentment that he works.[24] Flem is successful because he understands society so completely and because he is willing to submit himself to the terms it enjoins. Flem's submission is, in reality, the perfect realization of the power of amoral behavior. The wanton and detructive nature of such amorality is fully realized when it turns upon itself to destroy Flem, the high priest, at the altar, the mansion.

Contemporary society, as Faulkner sees it, creates and suffers from the Snopeses. Conventional social standards do not control the Snopeses because social conventions do not attest to any truth of the human heart, do not testify to the immortal soul of Man. Instead society is completely ruthless and inhuman because finance capitalism, economic brigandage, and mechanization have depersonalized man as a whole. His associations are built upon financial contracts rather than the "communal anonymity of brotherhood". Flem, in his repudiation of all human values, is perpetuating the society envisioned by men like Sutpen, a society narrowly restricted by a design, a society that will offer up a human sacrifice in order to maintain the *status quo*, the pretentious symbols of gain and power. Both of these men are fantastic careerists intent on self-fulfillment at society's cost. Sutpen's grand design and Flem's mean design are destructive threats to man because they seek to force or manipulate men in terms of a social letter of the law that allows no truth of the heart. Sutpen uses sheer courage and force as a destructive force; Flem Snopes uses cunning, deceit, and a character devoid of moral standard to infect the village and the town.

In conclusion, I should like to point out how fully Flem embodies all of the evils and destructive power described at the outset of this chapter. In Jasper's terms Flem lacks all sense of historical continuity with past or future; consequently, Flem does not remain man – he is more animal. In addition, Flem effectively pictures the destruction of what Wirth refers to as "the bases of social solidarity" because he continually "substitutes secondary for primary contacts" and his acts constantly weaken the "bonds of kinship". Flem is as soulless as the modern corpora-

[24]   Marcus, *Snopes Revisited*, p. 440.

tion cited by Wirth. Furthermore, Flem flowers in Jefferson, the Protestant ethos that Fromm describes with its middle class morality and its "fierce economic battle in which each one fights against everybody else".

As the quotation at the outset of this chapter indicates, Faulkner is not afraid of an urban civilization as such, but he does fear the type of mentality associated with its capitalistic centers. The modern Protestant era has produced the Flem Snopes type, and this type moves to the city "to find more people to use". Therefore, in Faulkner's view of modern, economic society destructive force is in human character rather than in physical environment. Faulkner defines this destructive force as predatory amorality because this constitutes soullessness for him. His aim, successfully achieved through the figure of Flem Snopes, is to depict the tragic effects created by modern man without a soul. And Faulkner makes this effort that he may aid modern man in search of a soul.

VI. THE DEFENDERS

There's a ... quality in man that prevails, ... there's always
someone that will never stop trying to cope with Snopes, that
will never stop trying to get rid of Snopes.

The impulse to eradicate Snopes is in my opinion so strong
that it selects its champions when the crisis comes. When the
battle comes it always produces a Roland. It doesn't mean they
will get rid of Snopes or the impulse which produces Snopes, but
always there's something in man that don't like Snopes and if
necessary will step in to keep Snopes from doing some irrepa-
rable harm.

Faulkner in the University [1]

When the Snopes trilogy is considered as a whole, it becomes
clear that the rise and fall of Snopesism is the theme. Snopesism
has been defined in the previous chapter as a predatory amorality,
destructive in nature. Faulkner dramatizes the conflict between
Snopesism and moral consciousness by opposing the Snopeses
with two dedicated men who battle them in every way: Gavin
Stevens, the county attorney, and V. K. Ratliff, the itinerant sew-
ing machine salesman. These Rolands, as Faulkner calls them,
engage the Snopeses in civic warfare and attempt to prevent the
abuses of power the Snopeses perpetrate upon the people of the
village and the town. It is significant to note right now that neither of these men is city bred or oriented; furthermore, the moral
power each possesses will be seen to be a quality of the heart
sometimes referred to as the soul.

Warren Beck describes the moral warfare of Stevens and Ratliff as the action of "disinterested interventionists", but I think

---

[1] Gwynn and Blotner, *Faulkner in the University*, p. 34.

to call them the defenders is more accurate and telling. Stevens and Ratliff are not disinterested in any way; they are subjectively involved with Jefferson and Frenchman's Bend and their people. It is true that they engage the Snopeses with no vested interests inspiring their involvement, but they do more than intervene. They engage and battle the Snopeses in all-out war which they recognize will be fought slowly and to the death. The designation, the defenders, connotes commitment and the qualities of soul that are so lacking in the Snopeses.

The Snopeses, as we have seen, represent a soulless, urban mentality that impersonally uses people in order to effect a private gain. In contrast, Stevens and Ratliff exhibit a compassionate response to man, a response which they have acquired through a long association with the land. The land has taught these men truths of the human heart – patience, commitment, and love, and they have applied these verities to the human situation. These qualities of character indicate Stevens and Ratliff belong to the "communal anonymity of brotherhood", an ideal of human fraternity first expressed in Faulkner's fiction through Ike McCaslin's ritualistic encounter with life in the big woods. Consequently, Stevens and Ratliff are capable of seeing men as "poor sons of bitches", a designation that is sympathetic as well as descriptive. They avoid losing faith in man and his affairs, for they avoid heartless associations and judgments. They understand that men are driven to self-protective and destructive actions because they are cut off from a spiritual center – the earth. Stevens summarizes his whole experience with the Snopeses with the statement: "The poor sons of bitches that have to cause all the grief and anguish they have to cause." [2] This final reaction of Stevens is typical of a prevailing attitude that characterizes him. It may be called "concern" or "involvement" or "intervention" as some critics designate it, but more accurately it is compassion, or – more simply – it is love that is engaged.

Since Snopesism is destructive, it is anti-life, and its encounter with life calls forth a champion who opposes it. "When the battle

[2] *The Mansion,* p. 430.

comes it always produces a Roland", says Faulkner. The instinctive response of the defenders typifies positive life because they
respond as a result of a consciousness and a conscience which
they possess. In other words, Stevens and Ratliff are "aware" of
the Snopeses and they feel "compelled" to respond to the threat
the Snopeses pose. When they respond, Stevens and Ratliff
"live". They live in themselves and on behalf of others, for it is
the nature of life and love to protect and perpetuate itself. It can
be seen here how ideally the role of the lawyer adapts to this
representation of character. The actions of a lawyer can be seen
as expressions of life and love because of the logical opportunities
of involvement in the personal and communal life of others. There
is profit in examining Faulkner's lawyer figure in some detail in
order to understand the consciousness and conscience of Gavin
Stevens that make him a champion.

Faulkner seems to have always possessed an interest in the
figure of the lawyer. In his earliest novels the lawyer figure is
Horace Benbow, who plays a part in *Sartoris* (1929) and *Sanctuary* (1931). Benbow is a man unable to cope with evil – a man
who does not have the moral power to withstand the sordidness
and injustice of immorality. Benbow is replaced by Stevens in
Light in August (1932), and Stevens remains the lawyer figure
in all the rest of Faulkner's works. Stevens is a man unsurprised by
and also unafraid of the ugliness of amorality and immorality.
Benbow did not possess the qualities of a Roland, so Faulkner
dropped him in favor of Stevens. Benbow is worth examining in
some detail, however, for his weaknesses and inability attest, in a
negative way, to the positive virtues required to defeat, or at least
protest against, evil.

Mr. James Brown suggests that Benbow's tragedy is self-defeat;
that is, he possesses an awareness of evil but is ignorant of what
is right.[3] Benbow is a weak moral agent because he does not know
what to do; to use Faulkner's words, he does not know how to
"step into" a problem. Benbow rather foolishly believes justice
will prevail because people will eventually discover the truth and

[3]   James Brown, "Shaping the World of *Sanctuary*", *University of Kansas
City Review*, XXV (Dec. 2, 1958), p. 138.

act righteously upon it. While he waits for a proper course of action to form, the forces of destruction consume him.

Everything about Horace, except his concern, suggests weakness. There is about him an air of a fine and delicate futility. "He is a lawyer", Faulkner says, "principally through a sense of duty to the family tradition." He is divorced from action, however, for he loves "printed words and the dwelling place of books", where he can retreat and contemplate "the meaning of peace". After a series of experiences with violence and immorality Benbow sadly realizes his world is shattered; the last words heard from him are "Less oft is peace. Less oft is peace."

In *Sartoris* Horace is involved in an affair with a woman who is cannily stupid, Belle Mitchell. She manipulates and abuses Horace, but he plays his part toward her "like the old actor whose hair is thin and whose profile is escaping him via his chin, but who can play to any cue on a moment's notice".[4] When he is not toying with Belle, Horace is blowing glass, an avocation that suggests his futility and ineffectiveness.

In *Sanctuary* Horace takes the defense of the accused murderer, Godwin, because he feels "a man might do something just because he knew it was right, necessary to the harmony of things that it be done".[5] However, the sexual violence involved in the case unnerves him; he begins to feel sexual desires for his stepdaughter; and he is amazed at the complexity of evil. In addition, he can get no information from Temple Drake that will help his client. The whole experience proves to be too much for him; he says, "I'll finish this business and then I'll go to Europe. I am sick. I am too old for this. I was born too old for it, and I am sick to death for quiet." Horace senses the abstract and ineffectual quality of his idealism, the folly of his life: "My soul has served an apprenticeship that has lasted forty-three years. Forty three years ... So you see that folly, as well as poverty, cares for its own." [6] As *Sanctuary* closes Benbow is seen as a defeated idealist unequipped to carry on a battle against evil, so one can well un-

---

[4] *Sartoris*, p. 194.
[5] *Sanctuary*, p. 331.
[6] *Ibid.*, pp. 313, 336-37.

derstand why Faulkner would drop the figure of Benbow. Faulkner assigns his role to another – Gavin Stevens – in order to present a picture of an effective moral warrior.

Gavin Stevens is not really the central character of any novel; the picture one gets of Stevens is a composite that must be gathered from all the stories in which he plays a part. Stevens is a native Jeffersonian and first and foremost a scholar. He is Harvard educated, a Heidelberg Ph.D., and he is quite unashamed of his Phi Beta Kappa key. After World War I, and a tour of duty as a stretcher-bearer, he returns to Jefferson, opens his law practice, becomes county attorney and settles down as a bachelor with his twin sister Margaret in a respectable, unpretentious frame house. He understands all of the people of Jefferson: the Negroes, the rednecks, the merchants, the sheriff, the Snopeses, the aristocracy, for he grew up with them in understanding and love, and he has dedicated his life to serve them. He often sits on the galleries with the farmers talking their language, even making deliberate grammatical errors in order to communicate with them on their level. Outside of his work Stevens has two projects, the education of his nephew, Chick Mallison, and the translation of the Old Testament into classic Greek. This latter project seems to represent a "disinterested scholarship" to Stevens since there is absolutely no practicality in the project whatsoever. In appearance Stevens is apparently undistinguished except for a shock of prematurely white hair. His most characteristic feature is his ability and desire to talk. Faulkner calls Stevens a "disembodied voice" and presents him as a compulsive talker; he explains, relates, informs, speculates upon everything. He has to "complicate things up" like Tom Sawyer – a figure he has some kinship with – in order to give them proper significance and make them worthy of human effort and achievement. Ratliff observes of Stevens' approach, "if it ain't complicated up enough, it ain't right". The reader is aware that Stevens uses his cushion of words to objectify events and place them into perspective for action.

Stevens shows an interesting development in the novels. He is characterized early as rhetorician in a classical sense; there is always in his words the search for relationships. By always talking about all events he keeps them in his consciousness; by speculating on the meaning of events he judges them according to conscience. Stevens undergoes a gradual growth in the novels that is reflected by the various ways in which he functions in them. In *Light in August* his words act purely as a summary of the story. In *Knight's Gambit* and in *Intruder in the Dust* he comments on the action much in the manner of a chorus. In *Requiem for a Nun, The Town,* and *The Mansion* he verbalizes the moral alternatives of action so that a proper choice may be made.

The book *Knight's Gambit* offers a good insight into Stevens' role in Jefferson. This book is a collection of whodunit stories, all of which involve Stevens either as defender or sleuth. The Knight's gambit is, of course, a chess move in which the knight is sacrificed in order to effect a larger gain. As county attorney, Stevens has the opportunity to be the knight of Jefferson, taking risks to preserve justice. In most of the stories Stevens sees crime and injustice as a violation of "the broad, heat-miraged land . . . the cotton and the corn of God's long-fecund remorseless acres, which would outlast any corruption and injustice".[7] The short story "Smoke" in *Knight's Gambit* is a good illustration of these points of sacrificial risk and violation of the land. In the story one or the other of Anselm Holland's twin sons is suspected of murdering the father to get the land. Stevens uncovers the real murderer, Granby Dodge, a man who does not know the land, cannot farm; he is "half a stock trader and half a lay preacher . . . and probably no better at either of these than at farming".[8] One of the sons, Virginius (the name is significant), is a real farmer, and he gets the land through Stevens' influence. Virginius wants to give half the land to his twin, a man to whom the land is "that damned farm", but Stevens steps in and says, "You just treat it right . . . Anse don't need any land." [9] Stevens sees that Virginius gets his reward, for Virginius possesses the right attitude toward the land – love. Stevens acts upon his judgments, confident that his knowledge of people is sound. He trusts man's relationship to the

[7] *Knight's Gambit*, p. 60.
[8] *Ibid.*, p. 7.
[9] *Ibid.*, p. 34.

land, for man's relationship to his fellows and the community depends on his relationship to the land. It is on the basis of this measure of men and events that Stevens is willing to take the risks and responsibilities of knighthood.

In the title story of *Knight's Gambit* Stevens represents the traditional South standing in opposition to the violent and criminal present, and his stand is so valiant he wins the heart of a princess. A bootlegger from New Orleans marries the daughter of an old time resident of Jefferson and rebuilds the family house to look "like the Southern mansion in the moving picture, only about five times as big and ten times as Southern".[10] It is later discovered that the bootlegger's wife, Mrs. Harriss, has been a young love of Stevens'; after her marriage she has two children and some time after that her husband dies. Mrs. Harriss does not allow money or travel to pervert character; she retains that "constancy, that imperviousness, that soft still malleableness which had lived ten years in the glittering capitals of Europe without even having to be aware that she had completely resisted them".[11] Mrs. Harriss is as unpretentious as her father, a man who loved and farmed his heritage. Each of them possesses a tenderness of spirit and a love of the soil. According to Stevens there are the characteristics of the "lowly and invincible of the earth" that will "endure, and endure and then endure, tomorrow, and tomorrow, and tomorrow".[12] Stevens takes a knight's risk for Mrs. Harriss by saving her children when they get into trouble; in the end he gets his own rich reward, Mrs. Harriss. By committing Stevens to this "early" marriage Faulkner saves him from the role of possible husband to Linda Snopes in *The Mansion*. Thus Stevens is shown to be capable of love as well as gallantry in his early appearances, and this characteristic is developed to the full in *The Mansion* where his love is greater than mere romance or sexual passion.

In *Requiem for a Nun* Stevens is more than a detective-lawyer-judge, more than a valiant knight; he is a high priest ministering at an act of redemption. In this sequel to the *Sanctuary* story, Stevens encourages Temple Drake to visit the governor and tell him the story of her life in the hope that he may pardon Nancy, the murderess of Temple's child. He badgers her into confession and contrition before the governor. Mrs. Olga Vickery has cleverly said, "Gavin Stevens, the 'Sage of Yoknapatawpha' becomes a Socratic midwife presiding over the moral dialectic which focuses on Temple Drake." [13] As will be remembered, Temple Drake's problem is that good and evil are just words without meaning, but Stevens, through his vitality and empathetic conscience, sets the stage for her "to recognize the sign, to engage in the moral dialectic and to make a living reality out of what has been too long merely a word".[14]

In the succession of roles just described, Stevens continually illustrates his involvement and power in the intricacies of the human situation. He is not overwhelmed by evil or its machinations despite the fact that he is sometimes amazed at its perversity. The variety of his functions further indicates his versatility and the range of responses he is capable of making. Up to *The Town* in Faulkner's fiction, Stevens derives his moral power out of knowledge deepened into understanding and love expressed through commitment, and his typical function is defending another. However, the threat of the Snopeses is something that Stevens feels personally, because the Snopeses are an amoral force striking at the structure of social order rather than particular victims. Stevens responds personally to this social threat because he is Jefferson – the defender, yes, but also its spirit, its traditions, its values. Stevens, along with two others like him, his nephew and Ratliff, act to save themselves and Jefferson from the Snopeses. In the Snopes trilogy Stevens' role expresses new depths of moral power in human character.

In their response to the Snopeses' threat Stevens and Ratliff represent man – enduring and prevailing man. They rise up and respond because "nobody else in Jefferson seemed to recognize

---

[13]   Olga Vickery, "Gavin Stevens: From Rhetoric to Dialectic", *Faulkner Studies*, II (Spring 1953), p. 4.
[14]   *Ibid.*

the danger".[15] Ratliff expresses the joy and strength in their engagement with the Snopeses when he reacts to their settling in
Jefferson:

No we got them now; they're ourn now; I don't know jest what Jefferson could a committed back there whenever it was, to have won this
punishment, gained this right, earned this privilege. But we did. So
it's for us to cope, to resist; us to endure, and (if we can) survive.[16]

Stevens and Ratliff see the Snopeses as a threat to all society. It
becomes the particular privilege of Stevens and Ratliff – this town
and country partnership – to respond because "there's a quality
in man that prevails ... there's always someone that will never
stop trying to cope with the Snopes, that will never stop trying to
get rid of Snopes".[17] Stevens and Ratliff enter the fray as men
willing to be tried and willing to be tested.

Stevens' testing as a moral warrior up to this point has always
been a test of wits; now he is tested in a variety of ways, each one
affecting personal desires on his part. It is only natural to expect
this depth of testing because Stevens must stand to lose more than
his reputation if his battle with the Snopeses is to be seen as a
struggle for survival instead of the civic responsibility of a do-
gooder.

First of all, Stevens' dedication to the cause is tested through
Flem Snopes's beautiful wife Eula. During Eula's eighteen-year
affair with Manfred de Spain, Stevens has been a dormant rival
"chewing his bitter thumbs out in the wings". Eula stimulates de
Spain at a dance to such an extent that he begins dancing with
her in an obscene manner. Stevens rushes in to defend Eula's
honor as well as the town's moral standards and gets thrashed for
his efforts. This public display of chivalry impresses Eula, and
she decides to try and use Stevens' fervor and passion to good
advantage. Here is a real threat to Stevens; if he accepts Eula he
will lose the privilege of attacking the Snopeses since she is one
of them. Eula urges him to forget his scruples in favor of a downright animal response: "You just are, and you need and you

---

[15]   *The Town*, p. 106.
[16]   *Ibid.*, p. 102.
[17]   Gwynn and Blotner, *Faulkner in the University*, p. 34.

must, and so you do." But Stevens informs her that if he acted upon those principles "I wouldn't be me then". Suddenly Stevens discerns the true purpose of her visit – she has come to buy protection for Flem. Stevens, however, will not be bought out of his moral war, and he refuses her.

We've all bought Snopeses here, whether we wanted to or not; you of all people should certainly know that. I don't know why we bought them. I mean why we had to . . . But nothing can hurt you if you refuse it . . . And nothing is of value that costs nothing so maybe you will value this refusal at what I value it cost me.[18]

In other words, Stevens has completely identified his own moral concern with that of Jefferson; he dismisses Eula with the remark: "Just say I represent Jefferson and so Flem Snopes is my burden too." Stevens emerges from his first test with greater strength; he has engaged a situation with only limited awareness, and as his understanding expands so does his moral strength. He does not act out of selfish interests but identifies his own best interests with those of Jefferson.

As the situation in Jefferson intensifies, Stevens takes a more open stand against Flem. Stevens tries to get evidence of Montgomery Ward Snopes's dirty postcard show, but Flem protects the public façade of the Snopes name by sacrificing his cousin to a bootlegging charge instead. Stevens then tries to get evidence on I. O. Snopes for deliberately allowing his mules to be killed by the railroad trains, but Flem drives his relative out of town. Finally the battle centers on Linda Snopes, a girl who is unaware that her real father is not Flem Snopes. Because she is not of Snopes blood but may become a Snopes because of environment, Stevens wants to save her from the enemy. He wants her to leave Jefferson and go away to college. Stevens feels "To save Jefferson from the Snopeses is a crisis, an emergency, a duty. To save a Snopes from Snopeses is a privilege, an honor, a pride." [19] Beck sees a great deal of significance in Stevens' action toward Eula and Linda – at least he interprets it in a significant way: "Snopesism most acutely affronts and unavoidably chal-

18 *The Town*, pp. 94-95.
19 *Ibid.*, p. 182.

lenges Gavin by its victimizing of Eula and its threats to Linda;
the magnanimity of Gavin's concern for both Eula and Linda,
resting in moral conviction, is the opposite pole to Snopes meanness. On this contrast the trilogy is poised." [20] The patterned contrast between the Snopeses' amorality ("meanness") and
Stevens' morality is employed throughout Faulkner's fiction both
within novels and between them. Therefore, Beck is quite right in
pointing out, at some point, that Gavin Stevens' engagement in
the situation of another, in this case Linda Snopes, is an expression of his morality.

The struggle over Linda Snopes and her liberation from Flem
brings the second volume of the trilogy to a close. It will be remembered that Flem threatens to tell Linda of Eula's love affair
– by making the whole thing public – unless he gets the bank
presidency from de Spain. Eula comes to Stevens for help in protecting Linda, and Stevens promises to watch out for Linda even
if he has to marry her. (In *The Town* Faulkner either ignored or
forgot that Stevens is already married.) Eula then believes she is
freed from the responsibilities of the situation. Her suicide provides Flem with another avenue to respectability – the monument. Flem will not release Linda until she has seen the monument installed. Stevens has supplied the monument in return for
Linda's freedom, and he fulfills his promise of protection by
sending her away to "college" – Greenwich Village. The war
in *The Town* ends in a stalemate.

Faulkner shows in *The Mansion* how Stevens' intervention on
behalf of Linda eventually pays off. Linda comes back to Jefferson a deaf war widow who has lost her husband and her hearing
in the Spanish Civil War. Linda arranges to have Mink Snopes
pardoned with the full knowledge that he will kill her father the
minute he is released. After Mink shoots Flem, Linda even helps
him escape and provides money for him to live on. Stevens is at
first bewildered at the apparent disaster that Linda has unwitting-
ly caused. But Ratliff reassures him by saying ". . . she knowed
all the time what was going to happen when he got out, that not

[20] Beck, *Man in Motion*, p. 113.

only she knowed but Flem did too".[21] Linda acts upon the principles Stevens has taught her, the principles that guide his own
life: "Just to hate evil is not enough. You – somebody – has got
to do something about it." Stevens' moral war has been carried to
its logical conclusion by his most fervent disciple. His love for her
as a person transcends romance and passion (he tells her "we
are the two in all the world who can love each other without
having to") – and symbolizes his greater compassion for man. It
is this compassionate concern that has stopped the Snopes' threat,
for in saving a Snopes from the Snopeses, Stevens activates the
machinery of retributive justice executed by Mink Snopes in the
name of humanity.

In an attempt to make the character of Stevens more believable
Faulkner assigns him several traits of character intended to hu-
manize him without weakening him. He is beset by a Prufrock-
like uncertainty in situations which are filled "with a thousand
indecisions which each fierce succeeding harassment would re-
vise". In *The Town* Ratliff has two one-sentence chapters designed to explain Stevens' inability to grasp a whole situation: "Because he missed it. He missed it completely." Stevens can miss the
point, and when he does it is usually because he is talking instead
of listening. As Ratliff says, "You never listened to nobody because by that time you were already talking again." Steven Marcus misses the point of Stevens' humanizing weaknesses and is
quite wrong when he says that "Stevens is a true solipsist . . . the
kind of monster who effaces the actuality of others by imposing
on them his own." [22] Stevens attempts to experience vicariously
the feelings of others that he may better understand them, but he
never orders their lives to increase his own sense of self-aware-
ness. Stevens talks about others and verbalizes their feelings because this is the way he learns. The rhetorical analysis of a situation and a person is his *method* of reaching meaning. Stevens'
need to talk in order to understand must be seen as a part of the
frailty that makes him the man he is. Marcus has looked only at
a portion of Stevens; he has adapted Chick Mallison's early view

[21] *The Mansion*, p. 431.
[22] Marcus, "Snopes Revisited", p. 439.

of Stevens without the balancing view that Mallison adds in a later perspective. In *Knight's Gambit* Mallison says that Stevens is "glib, familiar, quick, incorrigibly garrulous, incorrigibly discursive, who always had something curiously truthful yet always a little bizarre to say about almost anything that didn't really concern him".[23] Mallison's later view is more balanced and reveals an understanding of Stevens that parallels that of the reader.

Because he is a good man, wise too except for the occasions when he would aberrate, go momentarily haywire and take a wrong turn that even I could see was wrong, and then go hell-for-leather, with absolutely no deviation from logic and rationality from there on, until he wound us up in a mess of trouble or embarrassment that even I would have had enough sense to dodge. But he is a good man. Maybe I was wrong sometimes to trust and follow him but I was never wrong to love him.[24]

Warren Beck believes that Stevens' mixed character is a realistic achievement that marks the trilogy as an artistic success. Beck writes that

Faulkner's men of good will and well-doing for all their bafflement, are those whose motion, ethically purposeful, gives the fiction breath and pulse and the pace of life, and whose principled intention most profoundly validates the composition as realism, a total realism, actual complexity, full of the knowledge of good and evil endlessly interworking in that magnitude to be comprehended only through the tragic sense of life.[25]

Beck's reference to the "principled intention" expresses in this context the action of the defender. It is his action – not always successful – that creates in the fiction a sense of a real order of life – a struggle of opposing forces, destructive and preservative, evil and good.

In summary, Stevens is Faulkner's most actively engaged moralist. He conceives of himself as the defender of the established moral order in Jefferson. Stevens sees the town and the tradition he defends has weaknesses of its own, but certain good citizens

---

[23] *Knight's Gambit*, p. 165.
[24] *The Mansion*, p. 230.
[25] Beck, *Man in Motion*, p. 97.

redeem the shortcomings of others. Stevens believes a community must have a moral order to endure; when the community is associated with "God's long-fecund remorseless acres", it absorbs principles of growth – a cyclic regeneration – that perpetuate it. It is for this reason that Stevens believes: "you simply cannot go against a community . . . You cannot stand against the cold inflexible abstraction of a community's moral point of view." [26] Stevens sees the Snopeses as a threat to moral order because of their predatory amorality. The great danger, as Stevens sees it, is that a community should come under the influence of people outside of the moral order founded in the enduring order of the earth. When Stevens fights evil he is fighting to maintain a patterned life cycle; this makes him a champion of the people, an expression of enduring man himself. Stevens' life is his dedication and service to others. Ratliff makes the point very clear.

He wouldn't never be free because he wouldn't never want to be free because this was his life and if he ever lost it he wouldn't have nothing left. I mean the right and privilege and opportunity to dedicate forever his capacity for responsibility to something that wouldn't have no end to its appetite and that wouldn't never threaten to give him even a bone back in recompense.[27]

Stevens' "capacity for responsibility" includes Jefferson and all of its people.

What Gavin Stevens is to the town, V. K. Ratliff is to the country. Ratliff does not have the education of Stevens, but he is every bit as keen and at times far more perceptive, because his associations with the land are more natural and of longer standing. Like Stevens he is engaged in a moral warfare with the Snopeses; it is he who alerts Stevens to the threat, for he has seen the Snopeses at work in the country long before they arrive in the town.

Ratliff is a character that Faulkner loves and one into which he has poured a lot of humane qualities. Faulkner says that he wrote *The Hamlet* ". . . because 'Spotted Horses' had created a character I fell in love with: the itinerant sewing-machine agent named Suratt. Later a man of that name turned up at home, so I

[26] *The Town*, p. 312.
[27] *The Mansion*, p. 163.

changed my man to Ratliff." [28] Faulkner imbues Ratliff with moral fortitude and a flexibility that enables him to accept progress; as a result Ratliff is a strong and adaptable opponent of the Snopeses. Faulkner's own analysis confirms this:

I would say that the one least troubled by change was the sewing-machine agent Ratliff. That he had accepted a change in culture, a change in environment, and he has suffered no anguish, no grief from it . . . he's in favor of change, because it's motion, and it's the world as he knows it, and he's never one to say, I wish I had been born a hundred years ago, or I'm sorry I was born now and couldn't have put it off a hundred years. Ratliff will take what's now, [sic.] and do the best he can with it because he possesses what you might call a moral, spiritual eupepsia, that his digestion is good, all right, nothing alarms him.[29]

That is, Ratliff's "moral and spiritual eupepsia" is a sign of good spiritual and physical health and these characteristics, Elizabeth Kerr feels, make "Ratliff, not Gavin Stevens, the ideal humanist because he is able to live in the world of man and maintain his flexibility and zest and humanistic values".[30] Faulkner presents him as a man who is "instinctively" good because justice and truth and respect and love have been bred into him as a result of his close association with land. He loves the very "sun and air which men drank and moved in and talked and dealt with one another in". In the circuit of business through the hills, people see Ratliff as a man "affable and courteous, anecdotal and impenetrable". However, it is through his contacts with Flem Snopes, principally in *The Hamlet,* that we come to our deepest understanding of Ratliff. Flem Snopes is a point of reference by contrast, for Flem's "inhumanely neutral amorality emphasizes the ethical acuteness of his opponents".[31] We see and understand and admire Ratliff the most when he is closely engaged with Flem. His human concern is then most apparent as well as his genuine folksiness and trust. But we also see he is not blind nor stupid, and we are comforted at this.

Ratliff is both identified and disguised by his speech. When he

[28]   Gwynn and Blotner, *Faulkner in the University,* p. 256.
[29]   *Ibid.,* p. 253.
[30]   Kerr, "Snopes", p. 78.
[31]   Beck, *Man in Motion,* p. 88.

is one of the group squatting in front of the crossroads store, he seems to do all of the talking, but actually he is "doing a good deal more listening than anybody believed until afterward". When he does speak it is in "a pleasant, lazy, equable voice which you did not discern at once to be even more shrewd than humorous". Ratliff talks his way around his sales route passing gossip and gathering information on the well-being of the community in general.

More people should have observed that Ratliff comes out of a long-standing convention in American literature. As a character type his roots go back to the Yankee peddler, and this association explains his nature and his humor. Miss Constance Rourke in *American Humor* describes the Yankee peddler in a way that closely parallels Faulkner's conception of this "itinerant sewing-machine salesman".

Overassertive, yet quiet, self-conscious, full of odd new biases, he talked – this mythical creature: that was one secret of his power... His slanting dialect, homely metaphor, the penetrating rhythms of his speech, gave a fillip toward the upset of old and rigid balances; creating laughter he also created a fresh sense of unity... He was a symbol of triumph, of adaptability, or irrepressible life – of many qualities needed to induce confidence and self-possession among a new and unamalgamated people.[32]

As Miss Rourke points out, in time the Yankee was more and more frequently shown against the western background. The "gamecock of the wilderness" and the Yankee peddler formed "a striking composite with a blank mask in common, a similar habit of sporting in public the faults with which they were charged, both speaking in copious monologues... both given to homely metaphor".[33] Ratliff, of course, embodies all of these qualities and is proof of Miss Rourke's statement that this outline of American character has never been lost.

In the early stages of his relationship with the Snopeses Ratliff experiences some trouble in understanding them, and when understanding comes, he resists his role as defender. Ratliff really be-

[32] Constance Rourke, *American Humor* (New York, 1931), p. 35.
[33] *Ibid.*, p. 67.

gins to know Flem during the long and involved goat episode between them. Ratliff tries to outwit Flem and collect a note Flem owes to a Snopes cousin. But Flem maneuvers around the payment, and Ratliff begins to realize just how crafty Flem is:

I just never went far enough he thought. I quit too soon. I went as far as one Snopes will set fire to another Snopes's barn and both Snopeses know it, and that was all right. But I stopped there. I never went on to where that first Snopes will turn around and stomp the fire out so he can sue the second Snopes for the reward and both Snopeses know that too.[34]

As Flem's power increases Ratliff becomes more troubled; when he is asked what is wrong, Ratliff responds, "Why nothing, what could be wrong with nothing nowhere nohow in this here best of all possible worlds." What really bothers Ratliff is the admiration for Flem Snopes in the village and the willingness of the folk to allow him to prey on them. He protests against the complacency of the people.

Snopes can come and Snopes can go . . . take your pick. What is it the fellow says? Off with the old and on with the new; the old job at the old stand, maybe a new fellow doing the jobbing but it's the same old stern getting reamed out? [35]

The village response seems to thrust upon Ratliff the role of lone defender – a role he resists at first. "I never made them Snopeses and I never made the folks that can't wait to bare their backsides to them. I could do more, but I wont. I wont, I tell you!" [36]

But Ratliff does do more; he takes two definite actions, one of which exhibits his strength, the other his weakness. First, he steps in and makes Lump Snopes take away Ike's lover cow; he enforces this move on the basis of pure strength.

I know . . . that the reason I ain't going to leave him have what he does have is simply because I am strong enough to keep him from it. I am stronger than him. Not righter. Not any better, maybe. But just stronger.[37]

This is a picture of Ratliff acting upon conviction that leads him to

[34] *The Hamlet*, p. 89.
[35] *Ibid.*, p. 164.
[36] *Ibid.*, p. 326.
[37] *Ibid.*, p. 201.

take risks. He acts upon what he believes is right. Ratliff's second action against Flem involves his attempt to best Flem in a business deal involving buried treasure on the old Frenchman's place. Ratliff falls for Flem's trap; he responds to the possibility of a bonanza, for he feels a victory may lead to control or defeat of Flem through shame. Flem gains Ratliff's half interest in a restaurant in Jefferson in exchange for the field. Ratliff is left with a worthless field. Ratliff is human too; he has been stung, and he now respects the serpent's cunning even more. Flem leaves the hamlet to take over the restaurant in town. Ratliff follows him there and joins forces with Stevens in the war.

Ratliff's role in *The Town* is very restricted; about thirty pages cover his actions, but though his actions may be limited, his influence is not. Ratliff is a source of information for Stevens. It is he who first alerts Stevens of the threat to Jefferson; it is he who continually tries to explain Flem's motives to Stevens. It is Ratliff who first discerns that Flem is after respectability, and he tries to alert Stevens to Flem's motives: "But when it's respectability he finds out he wants and has got to have, there aint nothing he wont do to get it and then keep it." [38] However, on the whole, Ratliff is out of his element in the town; the action falls to Stevens. He observes, he judges, he laments and all of these actions are directed toward Stevens in his role as Jefferson's defender.

In *The Mansion* Ratliff's role is even more restricted; he narrates but three of the eighteen chapters. He is prominent in the story as a background figure; he is the narrator who fills in some of the events that happened in *The Hamlet*. In retelling the story of Eula's marriage and the episode of the spotted horses Ratliff adds a new perspective, but very little information. He is a participator of the action in *The Town* and *The Mansion* but not an initiator. He plays the role of loyal supporter and historian. However, with Stevens he supplies the concern and response that help defeat the Snopeses.

To conclude, the lawyer Gavin Stevens and the sewing-machine salesman, V. K. Ratliff, are humane and loving men dedicated to preserving worthwhile traditions. Faulkner depicts them as human

[38] *The Town*, p. 259.

beings subject to error and to the desires of the flesh; however, they seek and obey the spirit of an enduring moral code derived from nature. They are folksy, talky, whimsical men who approach life and people with a zest, a reverence, and a respect. They are naive at times since they are astonished at the perversity of the Snopeses amorality, but they are never overwhelmed. They lose battles, but they win the war. They fight a retarding action in the battle with Flem Snopes until Flem is destroyed by the perverseness of his own amorality. Ratliff is a man from the country whose morality is instinctive; Stevens is a town boy whose morality is acquired. Together these men form a team effort of moral attack and counter-attack that effectively save the hamlet and the town and the people from Snopesism.

As men Stevens and Ratliff are morally powerful because they possess the "verities of the human heart", which are the qualities of soul totally absent in the Snopeses.

The verities of the human heart. They are courage, honor, pride, compassion, pity. That they are not virtues, or one doesn't try to practice them, in my opinion, simply because they are good. One practices – tries to practice them simply because they are the edifice on which the whole history of man has [been] founded and by means of which his – as a race he has endured this long ... That is, they are the verities to be practiced not because they are virtue but because that's the best way to live in peace with yourself and your fellows.[39]

Stevens and Ratliff live in the truth of the human heart because to them the truth is "there" and cannot be denied. Theirs is not the dollar morality of Babbittry or Benjamin Franklin. That is, they do not "practice" virtue in order to gain their fortune. They are "good" because to be good is to be true. Snopes "respectability" is the modern equivalent of Poor Richard's *Way to Wealth*. Furthermore, Stevens and Ratliff save themselves, their fellow men and their community from the devastation of Snopesism because they act in the living present – they engage evil in order to expose and defeat it. Since they act out the best part of their humanity, they act in behalf of man. Their endurance is their victory, for Faulkner feels if the good white man can only learn to endure he shall prevail.

[39]   Gwynn and Blotner, *Faulkner in the University*, pp. 133-34.

VII. FAITH AND THE WORLD

Remember, the writer must write of his background. He must write out of what he knows, and the Christian legend is a part of any Christian's background. . . . I grew up with that . . . it's just there. It has nothing to do with how much of it I might believe or disbelieve — it's just there.[1]

Faulkner in the University

I believe that man will not merely endure: he will prevail. He is immortal, not because he alone among creatures has an inexhaustible voice but because he has a soul, a spirit capable of compassion and sacrifice and endurance.[2]

The Nobel Prize Speech

In *Bread and Wine* Silone has his disguised priest come to the realization that what man needs is to sit and talk long and quietly with his fellow man, for in this way a new age — "the kingdom of God" — may be ushered in. Faulkner shares the same point of view; both men look hopefully to the operation of a new force in the modern world — the force of brotherly love that results from faith in man. Silone's hope that "the age of the Holy Spirit" will replace the age of law is a condition Faulkner believes can be realized if man will stand against evil in behalf of other men. The intent of almost all Faulkner's fiction since "The Bear" has been to assert the hope for a new age. This perspective has not always characterized his writing. In 1939 Sartre said that Faulkner writes as though men were completely without a future; everything looked backward. He noted that reading Faulkner was like watching a road flowing away while looking out of the rear window of a

[1] Gwynn and Blotner, *Faulkner in the University*, p. 86 .
[2] Faulkner, *The Nobel Prize Speech*, Quoted in full in O'Connor, *The Tangled Fire of William Faulkner*, pp. 147-48.

moving car.[3] However, Faulkner's late fiction has caused critics like Henri Peyre to call him "prophetic" because he accurately diagnoses the condition of the times ("the tragic era of incomprehensible violence and inhumanity to man") and calls for a change of conditions in the future.[4] And Claude-Edmonde Magny has even termed Faulkner the greatest of the prophetic writers because his myth is so nearly universal and forward-looking.[5] His vision – faith prevailing in the world – is a resolution of the warring entities that characterize non-spiritual life; in American terms it is what Silone hopes will come to Italy and Europe. It is Faulkner's conception of a redemptive faith which he has discovered through a dialectic and progressive consideration of destructive and creative force.

Requiem for a Nun introduces Faulkner's approach to faith. In this book he attempts to dramatize the ideas about man, evil, and belief, that are embryonic in the novels of the late forties. The world of *Sanctuary* is recapitulated by Temple Drake as she gives a complete description of the acts of evil in her past. Because she recognizes that she has started the series of events that have led Nancy to murder her child, she desires to confess her guilt in the hope of saving the Negress from death. Temple is willing to do this because with Stevens' help she is learning to judge her own actions. Actually, she sees now that her whole problem has been an unawareness of what constitutes evil. When she is confessing to the governor, Temple explains that evil has replaced God as a direction-giver; since God is unknown to her she feels there is no means of identifying evil by contrasting it with an absolute.

I've got to say it all, or I wouldn't be here. But unless I can still believe that you might say yes, I don't see how I can. Which is another *touché* for somebody: God, maybe – if there is one. You see? That's what's so terrible. We don't even need Him. Simple evil is enough.[6]

[3]   Jean-Paul Sartre, "Time in Faulkner: *The Sound and the Fury*", in *Two Decades of Criticism*, ed. Frederick Hoffman and Olga Vickery, pp. 180-88.
[4]   Henri Peyre, *The Contemporary French Novel* (New York, 1955), p. 275.
[5]   Claude-Edmonde Magny, *L'Âge du Roman Américain* (Paris, 1948), cited by Lewis, *The Picaresque Saint*, p. 188.
[6]   *Requiem for a Nun*, pp. 128-29.

Temple needs evil to find "reality", but she has no way to translate the reality into purposeful behavior. All she can do is continually disobey, for that is the only sure way to feel she is really living.

She just had unbounded faith that her father and brothers would know evil when they saw it, so all she had to do was, do the one thing which she knew they would forbid her to do if they had the chance. And they were right about the evil, and so of course she was right too.[7]

Thus Faulkner elucidates Temple's past actions as a quest for evil. The next idea he introduces in the novel is that suffering helps identify evil and at the same time provides an avenue of atonement.

Temple comes to see that her confessional act is but a stage leading to the redemptive process of suffering. She tells the governor:

What we came here and waked you up at two o'clock in the morning for is just to give Temple Drake a good fair honest chance to suffer – you know: just anguish for the sake of anguish, like that Russian or somebody who wrote a whole book about suffering, not suffering for or about anything, just suffering.[8]

Stevens develops this Faulknerian concept of suffering a little further when he interprets a Bible verse on suffering and children.

God either would not or could not – anyway, did not – save innocence just because it was innocent; that when He said 'Suffer little children to come unto Me' He meant exactly that: He meant suffer; that the adults, the fathers, the old in and capable of sin, must be ready and willing – nay eager – to suffer at any time, that the little children shall come to Him unanguished, unterrified, undefiled.[9]

The novel is suggesting here that suffering is part of the world order of repentance. Temple then adds the next logical step in the process: good comes out of evil. "Oh yes I know that answer too; that was brought out tonight too: that a little child shall not suffer in order to come unto Me. So good can come out of evil."

[7] *Ibid.*, p. 136.
[8] *Ibid.*, p. 133.
[9] *Ibid.*, p. 163.

Stevens goes on to summarize the relationship between good and evil and suffering by saying, "It not only can, it must." [10] Suffering is thus understood to be the means of establishing the good; Faulkner's next step is to relate suffering to the concept of salvation.

The mission to the governor fails; he refuses to change the sentence, so Temple and Stevens decide to visit the condemned Nancy in jail. Though she is about to suffer the death penalty for her crime, Nancy says, "But you got to trust Him. Maybe that's your pay for the suffering." Temple asks, "Whose suffering and whose pay? Just each one's for his own?" Nancy explains, "Everybody's. All suffering. All poor sinning man's." Stevens humbly asks the enlightened Negro prostitute, "The salvation of the world is in man's suffering. Is that it?" Nancy responds, "Yes sir." [11] Thus the panacea for evil (sin) is suffering, and suffering is the means to a social salvation. Nancy next leads Temple and Stevens to the idea that undifferentiated belief is greater than mere hope and sustains the individual with an unfaltering trust. Stevens asks Nancy, "You mean when you have salvation, you don't have hope?" Nancy answers, "You don't even need it. All you need, all you have to do, is just believe." "Believe what?" asks Stevens, and Nancy says, "Just believe." [12] Some time later Temple also asks Nancy what to believe, and Nancy's last word is: "I don't know. But I believe." [13] What Stevens and Temple have learned, therefore, is that an undifferentiated belief is a faith or a trust in belief itself which one is led to adopt as a result of suffering.

Practically every critic who has opened *Requiem for a Nun* considers the ideas of good and evil, suffering, and belief to be weakly defined in this novel. The emphasis upon Nancy's great statement "Just believe" is on the first word, and this emphasis establishes the idea that the end or object of faith is unimportant as long as one is in the state or attitude of belief. This empty

---

[10]   *Ibid.*, p. 208.
[11]   *Ibid.*, p. 276.
[12]   *Ibid.*, pp. 272-73.
[13]   *Ibid.*, p. 281.

affirmation really worries Walter Slatoff who says, "The emphasis on Nancy's sacrifice and devout faith provides the book with a strong affirmative note, but Faulkner leaves in considerable doubt just what is being affirmed apart from the idea that man is capable of self-sacrifice and of enduring pain." [14] On the other hand, consider this statement by Hyatt Waggoner: "Nancy goes straight to the heart of Apostolic preaching when she distinguishes between the *didache* and *kerygma* and makes the *didache* dependent upon the *kerygma*: precisely the Pauline order, of course." [15] Waggoner is reading too much into Nancy's statements; he assigns to her a depth of primitive understanding she is not entitled to. Slatoff is right. Faulkner intends an affirmative, religious note; but what is being affirmed is quite vague and for two good reasons. First, Faulkner has not clearly defined the nature of evil for Temple Drake. Temple is almost browbeaten into the admission she did wrong, because she cannot understand who or what she has sinned against. Because the nature of her violation is vague, so is the nature of the suffering and belief she should submit to. Secondly, Faulkner was spending most of the years between 1944 and 1953 on *A Fable*, and one gets the impression he wrote *Requiem for a Nun* as a diversion, which may explain its lack of clear definition. In any event, *Requiem for a Nun* is a prolegomenon to *A Fable* in the order of Faulkner's fiction because it introduces spiritual concepts of faith and man, and it employs the Christian background in a mythic way. *Requiem for a Nun* is also a very good illustration of how Faulkner, or any other writer, may use the Christian legend as a part of his background "just because it's there". But for all its weaknesses the book does show how Faulkner has definitely moved to a point of view that can be described as "religious" or "spiritual", depending on how the word is understood. This much may be said clearly: Faulkner is working with the idea that personal salvation is related to belief, but we should note that the belief he advocates at this point does no more than enable one to "endure".

Faulkner voiced more of his ideas on belief in three public pro-

14   Slatoff, *Quest for Failure*, p. 210.
15   Waggoner, *From Jefferson to the World*, p. 224.

nouncements, (1) a commencement address at his daughter's graduation exercise, (2) the Nobel Prize speech and (3) the discussions with the Japanese people at Nagano. The thoughts Faulkner expressed in these talks develop some of the things he said in *Requiem for a Nun* and are a presage of many of the ideas that he attempts to dramatize in *A Fable*. At his daughter's commencement Faulkner, among other things, said the following:

> Our danger is the forces of the world today which are trying to use man's fear to rob him of his individuality, his soul, trying to reduce him to an unthinking mass by fear and bribery ... for their own aggrandisement and power, or because they themselves are baffled and afraid, afraid of, or incapable of, believing in man's capacity for courage and endurance and sacrifice.
>
> That is what we must resist, if we are to change the world for man's peace and security. It is not men in the mass who can and will save Man. It is Man himself, created in the image of God so that he shall have the power and the will to choose right from wrong, and be able to save himself because he is worth saving; Man, the individual man and woman, who will refuse always to be tricked or frightened or bribed into surrendering, not just the right but the duty too, to choose between justice and injustice, courage and cowardice, sacrifice and greed, pity and self.[16]

This speech is an accurate summary of what Faulkner has come to believe about Man – and note too that it is Faulkner's idea to capitalize the word *man* when he wishes to designate mankind. Faulkner feels that those who believe in "man's capacity for courage and endurance and sacrifice" can (1) throw off fears, (2) experience self-realization, (3) save themselves and (4) change the world. It is very easy to see how these ideas are an enlargement of Faulkner's earlier concept of belief. Pointless suffering and undefined belief, as dogmas of endurance, are succeeded by a faith centered specially upon Man (mankind), for to simply endure is not enough; Man must prevail, and he prevails by adding works to faith. The stasis implied by the stoical acceptance of suffering and belief now becomes an active resistance "if we are to change the world for man's peace and security". Faulkner believes in the value of resistance because of a hereto-

[16]   Cited by O'Connor, *The Tangled Fire of William Faulkner*, pp. 156-57.

fore unstated belief in the origin and worth of Man, which is well expressed in this speech and even more eloquently developed in the now famous Nobel Prize speech.

After Faulkner acknowledged the Nobel award as a recognition of a life's work during which he tried to create something "out of the materials of the human spirit . . . which did not exist before", he went on to state that "Our tragedy today is a general and universal fear." As a result of this fear, the writer, he said, should write of the "problems of the human heart in conflict with itself" in order to establish "the old verities and truths of the heart". After saying these things Faulkner used the pinnacle of fame to go on to a personal confession of faith in man and in a writer's responsibility:

Until he relearns these things, he will write as though he stood alone and watched the end of man . . . It is easy enough to say that man is immortal simply because he will endure; that when the last ding-dong of doom has clanged and faded from the last worthless rock hanging tideless in the last red and dying evening, that even then there will be one more sound: that of his puny inexhaustible voice, still talking. I refuse to accept this. I believe that man will not merely endure: he will prevail. He is immortal, not because he alone among creatures has an inexhaustible voice but because he has a soul, a spirit capable of compassion and sacrifice and endurance. The poet's, the writer's, duty is to write about these things. It is his privilege to help man endure by lifting his heart, by reminding him of the courage and honor and hope and pride and compassion and pity and sacrifice which have been the glory of his past. The poet's voice need not merely be the record of man; it can be one of the props, the pillars to help him endure and prevail.[17]

Again it is easy to see that Faulkner now expects more than man's endurance as a symbol of his nature. The new emphasis is that man may now *prevail* because of a specific faith in immortality, and such faith is a symbol of the nobility of his nature.

In his response to the Japanese people who were asking him questions, Faulkner reiterates some of the same concepts, but for the first time, in this context, he introduces the idea of God and the soul. "Man has a Soul", he says, "that aspires towards what

[17] *Ibid.*, pp. 147-48.

we call God." [18] But he quickly asserts that man's belief must be in himself.

> I do believe in man and his capacity for [advancement] ... That he still wishes, desires, wants to do better than he knows he can, and [that] occasionally he does do a little better than anybody expects of him ... that man is tough, that nothing, nothing – war, grief, hopelessness, despair – can last as long as man himself can last; that man himself will prevail over all of his anguishes, provided he will make the effort to ... believe in man and in hope – to seek not for a mere crutch to lean on, but to stand erect on his own feet by believing in hope and in his own toughness and endurance.[19]

Because of man's immortal nature, "Disaster is good for [him] ... If it does nothing else it reminds him who he is, what he is." [20] Faulkner also told the Japanese that the individual man who believes in himself is the one likely to protest and do something against evil. "It's that single voice, that's the important thing ... I think the salvation of man is in his individuality, that he has got to believe that he is important [as an individual of integrity] and not as a group." [21] This is why "anyone can save anyone from injustice if he just will, if he just tries, just raises his voice".[22] Therefore, Faulkner believes "to theorize about an evil is not enough. Someone, somewhere must do something about it".[23] It comes quite clear here: man's salvation is in his individuality; he must have faith in his own importance. That is, man must have faith in himself in order to have faith in Mankind. Action follows such a faith.

These public pronouncements are the response of a literary celebrity who is forced to state a creed because of public interest and curiosity. One feels the courteous Southern gentleman acceding to these requests for information with a little reluctance. The writer feels more at ease embodying his principles in a fictional world. *A Fable* is Faulkner's earnest attempt to do just that.

[18] Robert A. Jolliffe, *Faulkner at Nagano* (Tokyo, 1956), p. 24.
[19] *Ibid.*, pp. 5, 186.
[20] *Ibid.*, pp. 37-38.
[21] *Ibid.*, pp. 29, 195.
[22] *Ibid.*, p. 76.
[23] *Ibid.*, p. 97.

During nine years of what must have been hard labor, Faulkner attempted to project dramatically his beliefs about man's immortal soul, his toughness, his fight against evil, and his prevailing in an allegory of war and the Christian religion. This work is undoubtedly Faulkner's attempt at a *magnum opus*, for he spent longer in writing it than any other book by far, and in it he attempts to bring together all of the themes of a lifetime. "The book", as Waggoner correctly observes, "is an intricate, multi-leveled, massively documented and sustained imaginative statement of Faulkner's opinions on the possibility of salvation for man." [24] This move is obviously Faulkner's exhaustive attempt to relate his definition of faith to the world.

The character and action of an unnamed corporal in the French army dominates *A Fable*. The action opens during World War I at the Western front on "Wednesday in late May in 1918"; on this Wednesday the corporal has led a group of men in a movement of passive resistance and has been arrested for this act. The corporal is condemned to death, and the last days of his life, from Wednesday to Sunday, are developed in an allegory of the Passion Week. The corporal has many similarities to Jesus. He has twelve disciples – his squad; his gospel is peace and love in opposition to war and fear; he attempts to establish the rule of heaven on earth; he is opposed by the ruling authorities; he is betrayed by a Judas for money; he has a perfunctory trial; he is executed; and he has an implied resurrection because his body is never found. In all of these allegorical events a natural explanation is offered, for this is the story of the son of man, not the story of the Son of God.

Immediately after his trial and condemnation, the corporal is brought in to face the General of the Armies, and the scene between them suggests the temptation scene between Jesus and the Devil. In the allegory the old General represents Lucifer, the fallen angel, and in the story he is also the corporal's father. This somewhat mixed role was devised by Faulkner to suggest "Satan's fearsomeness, that he could usurp the legend of God and then

[24] Waggoner, *From Jefferson to the World*, p. 226.

discard God. That's why God feared him." [25] In the manner of
Satan the General offers the corporal three temptations (life,
liberty, and the pursuit of happiness – he is tempting an American messiah) if he will give up his cause. In the manner of Jesus
the corporal refuses the temptations because of his love of man.
"I give you liberty", says the General, and the corporal responds,
"To desert them?" The General then offers the earth, and again
the corporal responds, "There are still ten." The General then
acknowledges "that they, not you, are the problem; not you but
they are what we are bargaining for". The General finally offers
life: "Then take life", but the corporal's final answer is still the
same: "There are still ten." [26]

The corporal and the General represent two different ways of
looking at man. The corporal believes in man's goodness and
spiritual possibilities; the General sees the evil in man and his
material limitations. The General describes the difference between
them:

We are two articulations, self elected possibly, anyway elected, anyway postulated, not so much to defend as to test two inimical conditions which, through no fault of ours but through the simple paucity
and restrictions of the arena where they meet, must contend and –
one of them – perish: I champion of this mundane earth which,
whether I like it or not, is, and to which I did not ask to come, yet since
I am here, not only must stop but intend to stop during my allotted
while; you champion of an esoteric realm of man's baseless hopes and
his infinite capacity – no: passion – for unfact.[27]

The corporal, however, maintains his view of man despite the
General's superior power, and despite the fact that the General
informs him man is fickle. Men, says the General, may love now
but they "will hate you – until they forget you. [They] will
curse you until they have forgot whom they cursed." [28] The General, nonetheless, is forced to respect the corporal's view and
comes to admit that both of them have a faith in man, but he
realizes that the corporal believes in the good in man while he

[25] Gwynn and Blotner, *Faulkner in the University*, p. 63.
[26] *A Fable*, pp. 345-50.
[27] *Ibid.*, pp. 347-48.
[28] *Ibid.*, p. 343.

believes in the evil. The General sees man's capacity for evil as a
sign of his true nature, while the corporal maintains the opposite
view despite some evidence to the contrary.

Faulkner attempts to reconcile these conflicting views about
man's nature by synthesizing them; one grows out of the other –
good comes out of evil – and surpasses it in power. The General,
who states the synthesis, begins by reviewing man's "deathless
folly" in the machine age. In a concluding statement he voices a
now-familiar doctrine of Faulkner's belief.

'I dont fear man. I do better: I respect and admire him. And pride: I
am ten times prouder of that immortality which he does possess than
ever he of that heavenly one of his delusion. Because man and his
folly –'
'Will endure', the corporal said.
'They will do more', the old general said proudly. 'They will prevail'.[29]

The two statements about man form a coordinate revelation of
faith. As the scene between the corporal and the General moves
to a close, Faulkner attempts to put across the idea that it is
necessary for man (good) to stand against evil, for that defiance
is what leads to ultimate victory. The corporal illustrates this by
spurning the temptations, and the General acknowledges the power of the corporal's defiance in his farewell remarks.

'Good night my child'.
'Good-bye, Father', the corporal answered him.
'Not good-bye', the old general said. 'I am durable too. I don't give
up easily either. Remember whose blood it is you defy me with'.[30]

The corporal's successful defiance of the General represents the
victory of good over evil, the triumph of spiritual value over material value, the establishment of the "esoteric realm of unfact"
over the "mundane earth". The corporal's defiance defines him
as an individual. To use Faulkner's words, he has overcome those
who "are trying to rob him of his individuality, his soul, trying
to reduce him to an unthinking mass by fear and bribery". The
corporal's belief "prevails" over the General's because it postu-

[29] *Ibid.*, p. 354.
[30] *Ibid.*, p. 356.

lates man's immortal soul and a life beyond this life which allows man to exercise choice in this world without fear. Man is able to discover his individuality, make a choice for good, suffer in sacrifice, and live on in immortality. The prevailing power of the corporal's point of view is summed up in his words to the General: " 'Don't be afraid', the corporal said. 'There's nothing to be afraid of. Nothing worth it'." [31] The synthesis of the views allows for a belief in immortality despite evil and folly; man is free because he is without fear; because he is without fear he chooses the good. Faulkner asserts that belief in man's immortality is a creative force that initiates preservative action in the face of a threatening world.

The corporal's victory over "the mundane earth" (man as material and evil) is followed by his victory over the ecclesiastical world (man a little lower than The Organization). After he leaves the General for the last time, the corporal is placed in a cell where he is visited by a priest who has been sent by the General. The priest's viewpoint is spiritually lifeless; he attempts to persuade the corporal to save his life, and he uses Christ's life as an analogy. He points out that it was not the power of Christ's life that converted the world; it was the power of the institutionalized church. "It wasn't He with his humility and pity and sacrifice that converted the world; it was pagan and bloody Rome which did it with his martyrdom." [32] The priest tries to convince the corporal that the life he possesses and is willing to sacrifice ought not be given over to death, for all that will come of that is "nebulous and airy faith". What is needed is ecclesiastical authority to define good and evil and morality. The church is more important than a person, for the church is:

an establishment, a morality of behavior inside which man could exercise his right and duty for free will and decision, not for a reward resembling the bedtime tale which soothes the child into darkness, but the reward of being able to cope peacefully, hold his own, with the hard durable world in which . . . he found himself.[33]

[31] *Ibid.*, p. 352.
[32] *Ibid.*, p. 363.
[33] *Ibid.*, p. 364.

The corporal does not accept or believe in the moral power of an organization, so he is unresponsive; however, the priest feels he may be convincing him that martyrdom means the loss of his cause. He begins to offer the corporal the same temptations the General offered: power, life, the earth. Suddenly news is brought to the corporal that one who has denied him three times has returned to be with other members of the squad. It strikes the chaplain "there are still ten" who will not forget the person of the corporal, and he realizes the emptiness of a systematized religion that forgets the value of the person. He asks the corporal to save him, but the corporal does not understand what he means (man must save himself). The priest goes out of the cell and a short time later commits suicide. His death is the death of mere religiosity. The corporal's triumph is the victory of spiritual belief.

The action that leads up to these events in *A Fable* presents three characters whose struggle to discover a truth about evil and man reinforces a central idea in the book: man must do something against evil in order to discover good. These three men are Gerald Levine, the romantic young pilot who seeks personal glory through war; the Norman, a quartermaster general who was a schoolmate of the General's; and the runner, an embittered officer who seeks demotion in order to be with the men. Levine and the Norman are men who believe in an illusion ("glory" and the old General); when they meet the real situation (evil) they suffer disillusion and defeat and death. On the other hand, the runner's seeming disillusion is really a mask for his love of man. After a series of experiences he leads a battalion of unarmed men into no-man's land and survives. He has joined actively on the side of good and withstood the worst that evil can do. He concludes that "Evil is a part of man, evil and sin and cowardice, the same as repentance and being brave. You got to believe in all of them or believe in none of them. Believe that man is capable of all of them, or he ain't capable of none." When the runner learns this, he says: "Thanks. Maybe what I need is to have to meet somebody. To believe. Not in anything; just to believe." [34] Because he believes, he acts and moves from disillusion to faith to survival. Thus the

34 *Ibid.*, p. 203.

runner is joined with the corporal (the unknown soldier) in the last scene of the novel, and his final words – "I shall never die" – are true of both of them and Mankind too, for faith is the victory that overcomes the world.

It is easier now to see that *A Fable* is an attempt to present dramatically a plan of salvation. Joseph Gold summarizes the meaning of the plan in this way: "A non-formal Christianity is Faulkner's answer to man's predicament. Love of man is the basis of it. All men must live by the same values. Christ is really a humanitarian everyman." [35] The negative meaning of *A Fable* seems more apparent to Dayton Kohler who says, "Faulkner's meaning, conveyed by the dead generals, the young airman, the Corporal, the suicide priest, the crippled Runner, the barbed wire of the prison compound, is plainly revealed: in war all men are crucified." [36] These are coordinate truths representing the good-evil nature in reality and man that Faulkner wishes to elucidate. Both meanings exist in the book, and there are more besides these, for Faulkner's plan of salvation is an intricate series of steps requiring man's reaction and action, instinctive and learned. Slatoff sees three themes in *A Fable*, (1) the various struggles within mankind between the common man and his rulers, (2) the problems of faith and sacrifice, and (3) the capacity of man to endure. To him these themes are a "summary of the ideas and attitudes which govern virtually all of Faulkner's works".[37] This, I believe, is quite right, and by analyzing these themes in detail, as we have done, we can now attempt to state the complete nature of Faulkner's prevailing faith.

The first step toward salvation is a recognition that the condition of civilization is chaotic because industrialism has sundered man from the land; social mores are corrupt; political and military powers refuse to recognize the individual. As a result, man is without roots or values and is gripped by fear. In order to transcend the chaos in civilization, man must have faith in his own individu-

[35] Joseph Gold, "Delusion and Redemption in Faulkner's *A Fable*", *Modern Fiction Studies*, VII, 2 (Summer 1961), p. 156.
[36] Dayton Kohler, "*A Fable*: The Novel as Myth", *College English*, XVI, 8 (May 1955), p. 478.
[37] Slatoff, *Quest for Failure*, p. 225.

ality, worth, and importance. With his own worth established, man must put aside fear. When fear is overcome, the outrage and horror of his condition will be recognized. Repudiation of the outrage in the past and the present follows, and then one "relinquishes" completely to the good and takes a stand for value by actively combatting evil. Suffering follows, but the suffering is endured because it is the price of faith. Faith is directed toward the suffering itself, belief itself, and man. As a result, individual man prevails, and if only one man prevails, Man will prevail; the world may be saved.

Obviously a new Faulkner "myth" is inherent within this material. The old mythic situation – the encounter of Southern man with anti-traditional forces, is succeeded in his work by an archetypical encounter of a man of faith with the world. The new myth is a contemporary projection of the traditional hero, and Faulkner has given him a new face and a new role to suit the condition of the times. Since the new Faulkner hero is a man of faith engaging the world, I designate this new archetype the myth of the faithful man. The Faithman in Faulkner is an archetype because he is a composite of all the creative forces necessary to save the tribe. An archetype, as Leslie Fiedler points out, preserves for us "the assurance which belongs to ritual alone: that which is done above, what is done here and now is done forever, what is repeated in time subsists unbroken in eternity".[38] This is precisely what Faulkner believes about the actions of the man of faith, and it fully explains the great emphasis in his later work upon the relation of faith to the world: that is, man with faith is archetypical of the best in the human condition that shall not merely endure but prevail; consequently, his acts become ritualistic for his fellows. The new myth of the faithful man is best illustrated in *The Mansion*, and we may now look at that novel and the hero, Mink Snopes, in the light of these remarks.

It would be easy, perhaps too easy, to illustrate the myth of

---

[38] Leslie Fiedler, *Love and Death in the American Novel* (New York, 1960). For a balancing view of myth see Richard Chase, *The American Novel and Its Tradition* (New York, 1957), pp. 237-46, and also his *Quest for Myth* (New York, 1949).

man in the characters of Stevens or Ratliff. Instead Faulkner chooses Mink Snopes, the cowardly, savage murderer in *The Hamlet* as a subject to re-enact man's growth from personal fear to individual manhood to representative humanity. It seems somewhat startling to consider a Snopes as a representative figure of enduring and prevailing man, but this is precisely what Faulkner feels can happen; this is what thirty-four years of living with the Snopeses has taught him about the human heart. Theodore Greene says, "Blasphemous as it may sound, he [Mink] becomes, in Faulkner's skillful hands, a kind of Christ figure, the symbol of humanity condemned, and able to drain its bitter cup, to face its own Golgothas, with unyielding courage and dedication." [39] The meaning is quite plain: if a Snopes can re-enact the legend of Man, anyone can. Nothing can destroy the redemptive spark of goodness in any man, even the most vile.

In *The Hamlet* Mink Snopes is seen as a small, cunning, furtive, rodent-like human being. He is indomitable and implacable, seething in rage, smoldering under oppression. He is bitter toward the whole human race because he is downtrodden. He beats his wife and children, sneaks about like a small animal, and refuses help from anyone. He is not mad at anyone in particular; he is "outraged" at the injustice of life itself that continually victimizes him. He despises his neighbor, Jack Houston, for his power and for his money. From Houston Mink receives the final outrage, for Houston demands an additional dollar pound fee for Mink's cow that he has boarded all winter. Mink has abandoned his cow on Houston's land knowing Houston will fatten it up during the winter; when he claims the cow in the Spring, he is unwillingly forced to work out the boarding fees; however, the demand for the final dollar is too much for him. After he kills Houston he becomes completely animal – living nocturnally, trusting solely to instinct, losing all rationality, and mutilating Houston's corpse. Finally he is hunted down with hounds and is sent to jail where he awaits Flem's help. Flem sends him no aid, and Mink is sentenced to

[39]   Theodore M. Greene, "The Philosophy of Life Implicit in Faulkner's *The Mansion*", *Texas Studies in Language and Literature*, 11, 4 (Winter 1961), p. 411.

life in prison. This is the character Faulkner has set out to redeem, and perhaps only Jason Compson and the high priest himself, Flem, are meaner than Mink. Mink spends thirty-eight years in prison, and those years parallel the thirty-four years Faulkner has lived with the Snopeses. While William Faulkner is refining his attitude toward man in Oxford, Mississippi, Mink Snopes is going through a metamorphosis in the Parchman state prison. The results demand a review of the whole case, and the novel opens in just that fashion.

Faulkner begins *The Mansion* by retelling the story of the murder from Mink's point of view. Houston is pictured now as a vindictive, "sulking, sullen" man who bullies and oppresses Mink until his demand for the dollar pound fee actually violates Mink's manhood. Mink finally finds it impossible "to live with himself and still keep on taking what he had from Jack Houston". He feels the decision to kill Houston is something forced upon him. "Houston made me do it", Mink says. "Houston's destiny", Faulkner says, "had actually and finally impinged on his, Mink's, own fate – which was another facet of the outrage." That is, Houston is using Mink as a scapegoat to release his vindictive rage at life's blind will. Mink sees Houston's impositions as a trial of his manhood to see whether or not he can stand up to the challenge of being a man. When Mink begins to see the depth of Houston's challenge, he begins to believe that Houston is a test set up by some sort of universal order. Thus Houston becomes a representative of all injustice and oppression toward the little man; he is seen as the anti-Man ordained by the order of Man to try Mink by inhuman acts. Mink, however, views man in the context of a cosmic justice which he describes as:

... them-they-it, whichever and whatever you wanted to call it, who represented a simple fundamental justice and equity in human affairs.

Because "they" represent justice, Mink believes that "He simply had to trust *them* – the *Them* of whom it was promised that not even a sparrow should fall unmarked." Mink accepts his testing, therefore, as a part of the order of life, and he sees a response as necessary to prove his affirmation of order.

Maybe in fact They were testing him to see if he was a man or not, man enough to take a little harrassment and worry and so deserve his own licks when his turn came. But at least that moment would come when it was his turn, when he had earned the right to have his own just and equal licks back just as They had earned the right to test him and even to enjoy the testing.[40]

"They" will have to prove to be as much of a man as he is, Mink feels, and then "They" will have to be as faithful to him as he has been to "Them". Mink believes if "They" fail him, "They" will not be able to live with Themselves, any more than he could live with himself if he kept on taking the injustice and oppression that Houston offered. According to Mink's rationale, therefore, all justice demands he suffer manfully, then strike down the tyrant, the oppressor.

At first Mink clearly separates his view of justice (it-them-they) from any notion of God.

By *them* he didn't mean whatever-it-was that folks referred to as old Moster. He didn't believe in any Old Moster ... Besides, he, Mink, wasn't religious.[41]

Eventually, however, Mink "takes back" his repudiation of "old Moster", for while he is in prison, he learns to accept the judgment of "They" and comes to see and call "Them" Old Moster. Mink combines his beliefs about the order of man and God because he sees these forces working together. This is a fact he had not observed before, but he gains this wisdom in prison. In youth he had given his faith back to God, but now:

I taken it back from God ... I didn't need no Church ... You don't need to write God a letter ... Because a man will learn a little sense in time even outside. But he learns it quick in here. That when a Judgment powerful enough to help you, will help you if all you do is jest take back and accept it, you are a fool not to.[42]

Mink achieves "faith" in "Them" – justice in human order – for he believes "they" will vindicate men. Thus he continually reminds himself of his new manhood when he is on the way to

[40] *The Mansion*, pp. 5-7.
[41] *Ibid.*, p. 5.
[42] *Ibid.*, pp. 99-100.

kill Flem: "Be a man, Be a man. You got to be a man, you got too much to do, too much to resk." [43] There is a lot at stake for Mink because now he is an agent of retributive justice. When Stevens learns Mink is out of prison and on the way to Flem's, he describes him as an agent of "destiny and fate". Mink becomes the agent of Man, because he is willing to act in behalf of "Them".

It is quite clear that Mink achieves many new characteristics as a result of his faith. "Parchman taught him how to wait", Faulkner says, for he had thirty-eight years to practice. Mink knows that the evil in Man, represented first by Houston and finally by his cousin Flem, is a part of "Them", but he has also learned that enduring is one way to combat evil.

Because patience was his pride too: never to be reconciled since by this means he could beat Them; They might be stronger than he but nobody, no man, no nothing could wait longer than he could wait when nothing else but waiting would do, would work, would serve him.[44]

Besides patience Mink adds to his faith, sense. Ratliff states that "Man aint really evil, he jest aint got any sense." [45] Mink's new sense is expressed in his willingness to throw off oppression in order to gain equality.

Not justice. I never asked for that; jest fairness, that's all. That was all; not to have anything for him; just not to have anything against him.[46]

A third characteristic Mink gains is a new respect for the land. He finally realizes that the earth is his friend, not his enemy. In Parchman Mink wants "Jest to get out of here and go back home and farm." [47] By the time Mink is released from jail his thirty-eight year apprenticeship has given him patience, wisdom, and love, and he is now a worthy representative of Man and the earth, and Old Moster.

43   Ibid., p. 262.
44   Ibid., pp. 21-22.
45   Ibid., p. 230.
46   Ibid., p. 106.
47   Ibid., p. 40.

Mink's killing of Flem and his own death are events that symbolize his union with Man and the earth. Mink kills Flem because
Flem is "inhuman", denying life by denying kinship. By casting
aside fear and oppression, by saving himself and acting as a man
in behalf of Man, Mink is able to overthrow one who would control man and use him for his own aggrandisement and power. By
an incredible set of circumstances Mink manages to get Flem
alone and on the second attempt with an old pistol, kills him.
Mink achieves the even break he waited for: "It was as if Old
Moster Himself had said, 'I aint going to help you none but I aint
going to downright hinder you neither'." [48] Mink has faith that
he will be able to kill Flem despite the circumstances. Old Moster
has not brought Mink this far just to deny him. Mink says, "I
don't need to worry. Old Moster jest punishes; He dont play
jokes." [49] Flem's death is justice vindicated, Mankind triumphant,
and Mink feels released; he has now joined Man; all that is left is
for him to unite with the earth.

Even as Mink is nearing the completion of his mission on behalf of humanity, he feels the attraction of the earth that only
ceases when it sets him completely free. Beck is correct when he
says, "Mink becomes archetypal in his awareness of the pull of
the ground on a man",[50] for Mink is ritualistically fulfilling a
drama that is as old as earth and man. Mink believes the earth is
always pulling at man from the time he is born.

The very moment you were born out of your mother's body, the power and drag of the earth was already working on you; if there had not
been other womenfolks in the family or neighbors or even a hired one
to support you, hold you up, keep the earth from touching you, you
would not live an hour.[51]

On the way to Flem's house Mink lies down to rest and "He
began to feel the slow, secret, tentative palping start as the old
biding unimpatient ground" begins to pull at him. After Mink has
acted on behalf of man he can lie down upon the earth because

---

[48]   *Ibid.*, p. 403.
[49]   *Ibid.*, p. 407.
[50]   Beck, *Man in Motion*, p. 179.
[51]   *The Mansion*, p. 402.

"he was free now, he could afford to risk it; to show how much
he dared risk it, he even would close his eyes, give it all the chance
it wanted". Mink has known of the tie between Man and the earth
"because a man had to spend not just all his life but all the time
of Man too guarding against it". Mink is re-enacting all the time
of Man, has re-enacted it, and now is free to join the folk of the
earth:

He could feel the Mink Snopes that had had to spend so much of his
life just having unnecessary bother and trouble, beginning to creep,
seep, flow easy as sleeping ... down, down into the ground already
full of the folks that had the trouble but were free now.

Mink mixes with "the folks themselves ... now, all mixed and
jumbled up and comfortable and easy so nobody wouldn't even
know or care who was which any more".[52] Thus Mink, along with
Stevens and Ratliff, joins the "communal anonymity of brotherhood" that Ike McCaslin discovered in "The Bear". Mink joins
Sam Fathers, Lion and old Ben who are "free in earth and not in
earth but of earth, myriad yet undiffused ... and, being myriad,
one".[53] This is Faulkner's earth where there is no death, not for
Sam Fathers, old Ben, Lion, or Mink Snopes: "dissolution itself
was a seething turmoil of ejaculation tumescence conception and
birth and death did not even exist". Mink joins the community of
Man in the earth, and because of what he has learned about himself and humanity, Mink is

equal to any, good as any, brave as any, being inextricable from
anonymous with all of them: the beautiful, the splendid, the proud
and the brave, right on up to the very top itself among the shining
phantoms and dreams which are the milestones of the long human
recording – Helen and the bishops the kings and unhomed angels,
the scornful and graceless seraphim.[54]

In the Snopes saga Mink Snopes has added another milestone to
the human recording, the mythic record of man's journey from
darkness to light, from individual man to the race of Man, from

[52] *Ibid.*, p. 435.
[53] *Go Down Moses*, pp. 328-29.
[54] *The Mansion*, pp. 435-36.

enduring to prevailing, from the body to the earth, from bondage to freedom.

The Mansion is a success as a novel because Mink Snopes is a successful dramatization of the faithful Man – one who "trusts in God without depending on him". This trust illustrates the mythic message Faulkner strives for, for in the myth of man religion is emancipated from God, and man makes and executes his own judgments. This ideal is expressed by Stevens who says:

So what you need is to learn how to trust in God without depending on Him. In fact, we need to fix things so he can depend on us for a while. Then He won't need to waste Himself being everywhere at once.[55]

Furthermore, *The Mansion* is a much better artistic recording of the myth of the Faithman than either *Requiem for a Nun* or *A Fable* because a sense of character and place is maintained throughout, and the use of symbol, such as the earth or prison, is smooth and appropriate whereas in *A Fable* it is forced and unlifelike. Mink's change of character is believable because his actions define the meaning of the change. The image of evil in *The Mansion*, the image that is so weak in *Requiem for a Nun,* is sufficiently strong to make the violence comprehensible, for Flem Snopes is a name in Faulkner's fiction that has a long background that can be counted on in *The Mansion*. In dramatizing the Snopeses as polar extrematies of good and evil, Faulkner employs the rich Yoknapatawpha material which serves him as a natural background for his new truths of the human heart.

A concluding word is now in order regarding Faulkner's presentation of faith in relation to the world. Most of the serious fiction published between 1950 and 1960 deals with this theme, and within this fiction there is a progressive enlargement of his idea of faith. Starting with a simple statement that "belief" is worthwhile, he refines and enriches this idea until belief can become an *auto de fé* with mythic dimensions. As his idea of faith deepens so do the consequences of its acts until their redemptive significance is extended from the person to the whole world. In brief, we may

[55]   *Ibid.*, p. 321.

say that Faulkner's works attempt to show that as "belief" is put to work in the world it moves mountains, for we have seen that the suffering of Temple Drake, the brotherhood sought by the corporal, and the justice due Mink Snopes are given vital meaning as the individuals act out their belief in fearless human terms. Finally, it should be noted that Faulkner dramatizes the effectiveness of faith in the world in terms of the creative forces present in his fiction from the very beginning. Faith is the substance of the enduring qualities that characterize Dilsey, Ike McCaslin, and Gavin Stevens. Faith is a composite of creative human forces, not a confessional act in terms of creed.

EPILOGUE – THE MEANING OF FAITH

Throughout his writing, Faulkner has illustrated that destruction in the form of violence or death may only be understood when it is set over against some form of creative order. Antithetical structuring of conceptual opposites and role inversions provide him with the means of examining the nature of reality. In this way Faulkner continually measures man against the forces that make up the conditions of his existence. This picturing of man under constant testing is Faulkner's way of writing about "the human heart in conflict with itself". Out of this conflict Faulkner has forged an individualized concept of faith, a concept formed dialectically.

We may now observe, therefore, that a complete statement of what faith means in Faulkner's fiction is to be gained through a summary analysis of the creative forces he affirms. First of all, it was noted that personal and social inflexibility is destructive because it refuses to adapt. The creative opposite is what Faulkner terms a "life in motion". Life in motion is expressed through the pursuit of a worthy goal; when one honorably pursues a worthy goal, he is exposed to the enduring, organic verities of life, which must be understood as truth itself. His chief symbol for "pursuit" and "life in motion" is the hunt. The second antithesis highlights a creative force in the contrast between lust and love. Lust is destructive because it is blind, selfish, and perverse. The creative opposite of lust is a special kind of love that is capable of enduring the change, the sin, and the sorrow that the furious motion of existence creates. A mother's love is the best representation of this kind of love, and the only appropriate word that can describe Faulkner's view of mother love is *agape*. The third and last antithesis described predatory Snopesism as destructive because it is without compassion or truth, hence it is soulless. The creative opposite is what Faulkner terms the "verities of the heart", i.e. "courage, honor, pride, compassion, pity".[1] To possess these passions involves one in an active engagement in combatting evil in the local community (the defenders) and the world (the corporal). All of Faulkner's characters who possess one or more of the creative virtues enumerated endure or prevail through belief. His ideal saints – the nun Nancy, the Christ-like corporal, the redeemed Mink Snopes – are heroes of the faith because they believe a very great deal, and they fearlessly act upon their belief to the extent of giving up their lives. They express the fulness of belief for Faulkner – faith – because of a total commitment to the creative forces of *pursuit, agape,* and *engagement.* The substance of faith in Faulkner's fiction is, therefore, *pursuit, agape,* and *engagement,* terms that have an existential ring to them signifying that Faulkner pictures faith not as a spiritual confession but as the master living force.

As this concept of faith tends to dominate the fiction of the last third of Faulkner's career, the nature of the fictional world also changes. Faulkner has moved slowly from regionalism to nationalism to internationalism in his fictional point of view. For instance, by the time of "The Bear" (1936) Faulkner no longer sees America in terms of the South; rather America is the focal point of the new world where the human race is given one more clear chance to live together in peace. Ike McCaslin expresses this thought:

Dispossessed of Eden. Dispossessed of Canaan, and those who dispossessed him dispossessed him and the five hundred years of absentee landlords in the Roman bagnios, and the thousand years of wild men from the northern woods who dispossessed them and devoured their ravished substance ravished in turn again and then snarled in what you call the old world's worthless twilight over the old world's gnawed bones, blasphemous in His name until He used a simple egg to discover to them a new world where a nation of people could be founded in humility and pity in sufferance and pride of one to another.[2]

[1]   *Go Down Moses,* p. 258.
[2]   *The Mansion,* p. 435.

And in *A Fable* (1954) America as a setting for the new world is succeeded by an international scene involving England, France, Germany, and the United States. Therefore, Faulkner has enlarged his theatre of action to "mythic" proportions: Jefferson has become "somewhere in France", that involves Jefferson, America, and all the rest of the world. Faulkner's fictional "world" has expanded to keep pace with his expanding concept of faith.

The emergence of the concept of faith in Faulkner's fiction has meant the emergence of a new concept of man, best illustrated by his uses of the Christ-symbol. This symbol has frequently been used by Faulkner to picture man as a victim of a society without faith; however, in recent years it has been increasingly employed to identify man as a prevailing force. In *The Sound and the Fury* (1929) Benjy is associated with Christ to highlight him as a defenseless victim. Similarly, Joe Christmas in *Light in August* (1932) is figuratively crucified. With the character of Ike McCaslin, however, Faulkner begins to use the Christ-symbol to suggest the possibilities of man's prevailing over the destructive threats in life. McCaslin in *Go Down Moses* (1942) is likened to Christ in that he prevails over the temptations of power and greed and adopts a solitary life of expiation. In *A Fable* (1954), of course, the corporal prevails over the worldly force of war and is likened to a resurrected and immortal Son of Man, the ultimate man of faith, the image of a universal savior. And with the publication of *The Mansion* (1959) and the use of the Christ-symbol Faulkner employs in it, there is no further doubt that he has come to the place of accepting man as a spiritual being fully capable of overcoming his frailties and his society by the power of faith. In the preface to *The Mansion* Faulkner says,

... there will be found discrepancies and contradictions in the thirty-four-year progress of this particular chronicle; the purpose of this note is simply to notify the reader that the author has already found more discrepancies and contradictions than he hopes the reader will – contradictions and discrepancies due to the fact that the author has learned, he believes, more about the human heart and its dilemma than he knew thirty-four years ago; and is sure that, having lived with them a long time, he knows the characters in this chronicle better than he did then.

In thirty-four years' time Faulkner has learned that even the Snopeses are capable of transformation through faith. His suggestion of Mink Snopes as a Christ-figure able to drain his own bitter cup and face his own Golgotha "equal to any, good as any, brave as any",[3] indicates Faulkner now believes that all men, even the Snopeses, are redeemable. We have, then, a new Faulkner myth, the myth of the faithful Man.

The characteristics of Faulkner's ideas and his form reflect, of course, his creative response to the situation of man as revealed by modern knowledge. Faulkner's conscious awareness of the complex human situation is apparent in this reflection about Jefferson, Mississippi, in *The Town.*

This miniature of man's passions and hopes and disasters – ambition and fear and lust and courage and abnegation and pity and honor and sin and pride – all bound, precarious and ramshackle, held together by the web, the iron-thin warp and woof of his rapacity but withal yet dedicated to his dreams.

His vision of Jefferson is the vision of contending forces: the warp of man's rapacity is the destructive force that is, in turn, crossed and recrossed by the creative force – the woof of his dream. By working with disorder in the human situation in terms of oppositions and paradoxes, Faulkner creates a picture of human life that believably suggests its ambiguities and its absolutes, and the conceptual antitheses that contain the meaning of Faulkner's fiction represent a dialectic method employed to discover and establish the panacea of faith. Faith that works within the human situation in terms of *pursuit, agape,* and *engagement* is a faith that Faulkner depicts as overcoming the world.

---

[3] *The Town,* p. 316.

BIBLIOGRAPHY

I. PRIMARY SOURCES

Faulkner, William, *Absalom, Absalom!* (New York, 1951).
——, *As I Lay Dying* (New York, 1946).
——, *Big Woods* (New York, 1955).
——, *Collected Stories of William Faulkner* (New York, 1950).
——, *A Fable* (New York, 1954).
——, *Go Down Moses* (New York, 1942).
——, *The Hamlet* (New York, 1940).
——, *Intruder in the Dust* (New York, 1948).
——, *Knight's Gambit* (New York, 1949).
——, *Light in August* (New York, 1950).
——, *The Mansion* (New York, 1959).
——, *Mosquitoes* (New York, 1927).
——, *New Orleans Sketches* (New Brunswick, 1958).
——, *Pylon* (New York, 1935).
——, *The Reivers* (New York, 1962).
——, *Requiem for a Nun* (New York, 1951).
——, *Salmagundi* (New York, 1932).
——, *Sanctuary* (New York, 1932).
——, *Sartoris* (New York, 1929).
——, *Soldier's Pay* (New York, 1926).
——, *The Sound and the Fury* (New York, 1946).
——, *The Town* (New York, 1957).
——, *The Unvanquished* (New York, 1938).
——, *The Wild Palms* (New York, 1939).

II. SECONDARY SOURCES

Adams, Robert M., "Poetry in the Novel: or, Faulkner Esemplastic", *Virginia Quarterly*, XXIX (Spring 1953), pp. 419-34.
Aiken, Conrad, "William Faulkner: The Novel as Form", *Atlantic Monthly*, CLXIV (November 1939), pp. 650-54.
Allen, Charles A., "William Faulkner's Vision of Good and Evil", *Pacific Spectator*, X (1956), pp. 236-41.

Anderson, Charles, "Faulkner's Moral Center", *Etudes Anglaises*, VII (January 1954), pp. 48-58.

Arthos, John, "Ritual and Humor in Faulkner", *Accent*, IX (Autumn 1948), pp. 17-30.

Backman, Melvin, "Sickness and Primitivism: A Dominant Pattern in William Faulkner's Work", *Accent*, XIV (Winter 1954), pp. 61-73.

Baker, James R., "The Symbolic Extension of Yoknapatawpha County", *Arizona Quarterly*, VIII (Autumn 1952), pp. 223-28.

Beach, Joseph Warren, *American Fiction 1920-1940* (New York, 1942).

Beck, Warren, "Faulkner and the South", *Antioch Review*, I (March 1941), pp. 82-94.

——, "Faulkner's Point of View", *College English*, II (May 1941), pp. 736-49.

——, *Man in Motion: Faulkner's Trilogy* (Madison, 1961).

——, "William Faulkner's Style", *Two Decades of Criticism*, ed. Frederick J. Hoffman and Olga W. Vickery (East Lansing, 1951).

Benson, Carl, "Thematic Design in *Light in August*", *South Atlantic Quarterly*, LIII (October 1954), pp. 540-55.

Bowling, Lawrence Edward, "Faulkner and the Theme of Innocence", *Kenyon Review*, XX, 3 (Summer 1958), pp. 466-87.

——, "Faulkner: Technique of *The Sound and the Fury*", Kenyon Review, X (Autumn 1948), pp. 552-66.

Bradford, Roark, "The Private World of William Faulkner", *'48, the Magazine of the Year*, II (May 1948), pp. 83-90.

Breit, Harvey, "A Sense of Faulkner", *Partisan Review*, XVIII (January-February 1951), pp. 88-94.

——, "William Faulkner", *Atlantic Monthly*, CLXXXVIII (October 1951), pp. 53-56.

Brooks, Cleanth, "*Absalom, Absalom!* The Definition of Innocence", *Sewanee Review*, LIX (Autumn 1951), pp. 543-58.

——, "Notes on Faulkner's *Light in August*", *Harvard Advocate*, CXXXV (November 1951), pp. 10-11, 27.

——, "Primitivism in *The Sound and the Fury*", *English Institute Essays 1952* (New York, 1954).

——, "Wilderness and Civilization: A Note on William Faulkner", *Partisan Review*, XXII (Summer 1955), pp. 340-50.

Brown, James, "Shaping the World of *Sanctuary*", *University of Kansas City Review*, XXV (December 1958), pp. 137-42.

Burgum, Edwin Berry, *The Novel and the World's Dilemma* (New York, 1947).

Campbell, Harry M., "Experiment and Achievement: *As I Lay Dying* and *The Sound and the Fury*", *Sewanee Review*, LI (April 1943), pp. 305-20.

—— and Ruel E. Foster, *William Faulkner: A Critical Appraisal* (Norman, 1951).

Cargill, Oscar, *Intellectual America* (New York, 1941).

Carter, Everett, "The Meaning of, and in, Realism", *Antioch Review*, XII (Spring 1952), pp. 92-94.

Chase, Richard, *The American Novel and Its Tradition* (New York, 1957).

Chase, Richard, "The Stone and The Crucifixion", *Kenyon Review*, X (Autumn 1948), pp. 539-51.

Collins, Carvel, "A Conscious Literary Use of Freud?", *Literature and Psychology*, III (1953), pp. 3-4.

——, "A Note on *Sanctuary*", *Harvard Advocate*, CXXV (November 1951), p. 16.

——, "A Note on the Conclusion of *The Bear*", *Faulkner Studies*, II (Winter 1954), pp. 58-59.

——, "Are These Mandalas?", *Literature and Psychology*, III (November 1953), pp. 3-6.

Conrad, Joseph, *Lord Jim* (New York, Random House, 1920).

Cottrell, Beckman W., "Christian Symbols in *Light in August*", *Modern Fiction Studies*, II (Winter 1956), pp. 207-13.

Coughlan, Robert, *The Private World of William Faulkner: The Man, The Legend, The Writer* (New York, 1954).

Cowley, Malcolm, "An Introduction to William Faulkner", in John W. Aldridge, ed., *Critiques and Essays on Modern Fiction* (New York, 1952).

——, ed., *The Portable Faulkner* (New York, 1946).

——, "William Faulkner Revisited", *Saturday Review*, XXVIII (April 14, 1945), pp. 13-16.

——, "William Faulkner's Nation", *New Republic*, CXIX (October 18, 1948), pp. 21-22.

——, ed., *Writers at Work: The Paris Review Interviews* (New York, 1958).

Daniel, Robert W., *A Catalogue of the Writings of William Faulkner* (New Haven, 1942).

—— and John L. Langley, Jr., "Faulkner's Critics: A Selective Bibliography", *Perspective*, III (Winter 1950), pp. 202-08.

Dominicus, A. M., "An Interview with Faulkner", *Faulkner Studies*, III (Summer-Autumn 1954), pp. 33-37.

Edel, Leon, *The Psychological Novel 1900-1950* (New York, 1955).

Edmonds, Irene C., "Faulkner and the Black Shadow", *The Southern Renaissance*, ed. Louis D. Rubin, Jr. and Robert D. Jacobs (Baltimore, 1953).

Elias, Robert H., "Gavin Stevens: Intruder?", *Faulkner Studies*, III (Spring 1954), pp. 1-4.

Emmanuel, Pierre, "Faulkner and the Sense of Sin", *Harvard Advocate*, CXXXV (November 1951), p. 20.

Feidelson, Charles, Jr., *Symbolism and American Literature* (Chicago, 1953).

Fiedler, Leslie, "William Faulkner: An American Dickens", *Commentary*, X (October 1950), pp. 384-87.

——, *Love and Death in the American Novel* (New York, 1960).

Flint, R. W., "Faulkner as Elegist", *Hudson Review*, VII (Summer 1954), pp. 246-57.

Flynn, Robert, "The Dialectic of *Sanctuary*", *Modern Fiction Studies*, II (Autumn 1956), pp. 109-13.

Foster, Ruel E., "A Further Note on the Conclusion of *The Bear*", *Faulkner Studies*, III (Spring 1954), pp. 4-5.

Frazier, David L., "Gothicism in *Sanctuary:* The Black Pall and the Crap Table", *Modern Fiction Studies*, II (Autumn 1956), pp. 114-24.

——, "Lucas Burch and the Polarity of *Light in August*", *Modern Language Notes*, LXXIII, 6 (June 1958), pp. 417-19.

Frohock, W. M., *The Novel of Violence in America, 1920-1950* (Dallas, 1950).

Fromm, Erich, *Escape from Freedom* (New York, 1951).

Galharn, Carl, "Faulkner's Faith: Roots from *The Wild Palms*", *Twentieth Century Literature*, I (October 1955), pp. 139-60.

Geismar, Maxwell, *Writers in Crisis: The American Novel Between Two Wars* (Boston, 1942).

Gerard, Albert, "Justice in Yoknapatawpha County: Some Symbolic Motifs in Faulkner's Later Writing", *Faulkner Studies*, II (Winter 1954), pp. 49-57.

Glicksberg, Charles L., "William Faulkner and the Negro Problem", *Phylon*, X (June 1949), pp. 153-60.

——, "The World of William Faulkner", *Arizona Quarterly*, V (Spring 1949), pp. 46-58.

Gold, Joseph, "Delusion and Redemption in Faulkner's *A Fable*", *Modern Fiction Studies*, VII, 2 (Summer 1961), pp. 145-56.

Green, A. Wigfall, "William Faulkner at Home", *Sewanee Review*, XL (Summer 1932), pp. 294-306.

Greene, Theodore M., "The Philosophy of Life Implicit in Faulkner's *The Mansion*", *Texas Studies in Literature and Language*, XI, 9 (Winter 1961), pp. 401-418.

Greet, Tom Y., "The Theme and Structure of Faulkner's *The Hamlet*", *PMLA*, LXII (September 1957), pp. 775-90.

Grenier, Cynthia, "The Art of Fiction: An Interview with William Faulkner — September, 1955", *Accent*, XVI (Summer 1956), pp. 167-77.

Guerard, Albert, Jr., "*Requiem for a Nun:* An Examination", *Harvard Advocate*, CXXV (November 1951), pp. 19, 41-42.

Gwynn, Frederick L. and Joseph L. Blotner, eds., *Faulkner in the University* (Charlottesville, 1959).

Hafley, James, "Faulkner's Fable: Dream and Transfiguration", *Accent*, XVI (Winter 1956), pp. 3-14.

Hardwick, Elizabeth, "Faulkner and the South Today", *Two Decades of Criticism*, ed. Frederick J. Hoffman and Olga W. Vickery (East Lansing, 1951).

Hassan, Ihab H., "The Victim: Images of Evil in Recent American Fiction", *College English*, XXI, 3 (December 1959), pp. 143-49.

Hayakawa, S. A., "Reactions and Words", in Harry Shaw, ed., *A Complete Course in Freshman English* (New York, 1959).

Hicks, Granville, "The Past and the Future of William Faulkner", *Bookman*, LXXIV (September 1931), pp. 17-24.

——, *The Great Tradition* (New York, 1933).

Hirshleifer, Phyllis, "As Whirlwinds in the South: *Light in August*", *Perspective*, II (Summer 1949), pp. 225-38.

180   BIBLIOGRAPHY

Hoffman, Frederick J., *The Modern Novel in America 1900-1950* (Chicago, 1951).
——, *William Faulkner* (New York, 1961).
—— and Olga W. Vickery, eds., *William Faulkner: Two Decades of Criticism* (East Lansing, 1961).
——, *William Faulkner: Three Decades of Criticism* (East Lansing, 1960).
Hoodley, Frank M., "The World View of William Faulkner", *Dissertation Abstracts*, XVI, pp. 3-14.
Hopkins, Viola, "William Faulkner's *The Hamlet*: A Study in Meaning and Form", *Accent*, XV (Spring 1955), pp. 125-44.
Hopper, Vincent F., "Faulkner's Paradise Lost", *Virginia Quarterly*, XXIII (Summer 1947), pp. 405-20.
Howe, Irving, *William Faulkner: A Critical Study* (New York, 1962).
Humphrey, Robert, "Form and Function in William Faulkner's *The Sound and The Fury*", *University of Kansas City Review*, XIX (Autumn 1952), pp. 34-40.
Jacobs, Robert D., "Faulkner's Tragedy of Isolation", *Hopkins Review*, VI (Spring-Summer 1953), pp. 162-83.
Jaspers, Karl, *Man in the Modern Age* (New York, 1957).
Jellife, Robert A., *Faulkner at Nagano* (Tokyo, 1956).
Jung, C. G., *Psychology of the Unconscious*, Trans. Beatrice M. Hinkle (New York, 1943).
Kazin, Alfred, *The Inmost Leaf* (New York, 1955).
——, *On Native Grounds* (New York, 1933).
——, "The Stillness of *Light in August*", in Charles Feidelson, Jr. and Paul Brodtkorb, Jr., *Interpretations of American Literature*.
Kerr, Elizabeth M., "Snopes", *Wisconsin Studies in Contemporary Literature*, 1, 2 (Spring-Summer 1960), pp. 66-83.
King, Roma, Jr., "Everyman's Warfare: A Study of Faulkner's *A Fable*", *Modern Fiction Studies*, II (Autumn 1956), pp. 132-38.
——, "The Janus Symbol in *As I Lay Dying*", *University of Kansas City Review*, XXI (Summer 1955), pp. 287-90.
Kohler, Dayton, "A Fable: The Novel as Myth", *College English*, XVI (May 1955), pp. 471-78.
Kluckhohn, Clyde, *Mirror for Man* (New York, 1949).
——, "William Faulkner and the Social Conscience", *College English*, XI (December 1949), pp. 119-27.
Kubie, Lawrence S., "William Faulkner's *Sanctuary*: An Analysis", *Saturday Review*, II (October 20, 1934), pp. 224-26.
LaBudde, Kenneth, "Cultural Primitivism in Faulkner's *The Bear*", *American Quarterly*, II (Winter 1950), pp. 322-28.
Lawrence, D. H., *Studies in Classic American Literature* (New York, 1953).
Lee, Edwy B., "A Note on the Ordonnance of *The Sound and the Fury*", *Faulkner Studies*, III (Summer-Autumn 1954), pp. 37-39.
Levin, Harry, *The Power of Blackness* (New York, 1958).
Lewis, R. W. B., *The American Adam* (Chicago, 1955).
——, *The Picaresque Saint* (New York, 1959).
Lewis, Wyndham, *Men Without Art* (New York, 1934).

Linde, Ilse Dusoir, "The Teachable Faulkner", *College English*, XVI (February 1955), pp. 284-87, 302.
——, "The Design and Meaning of *Absalom, Absalom!*", *PMLA*, LXX (December 1955), pp. 887-912.
Lisca, Peter, "*The Hamlet:* Genesis and Revisions", *Faulkner Studies*, III (Spring 1954), pp. 5-13.
——, "Some New Light on Faulkner's *Sanctuary*", *Faulkner Studies*, II (Spring 1953), pp. 5-9.
Litz, Walton, "Genealogy as Symbol in *Go Down Moses*", *Faulkner Studies*, I (Winter 1952), pp. 49-53.
——, "William Faulkner's Moral Vision", *Southwest Review*, XXXVII (Summer 1952), pp. 200-09.
Lowrey, Perrin, "Concepts of Time in *The Sound and the Fury*", *English Institute Essays 1952* (New York, 1954).
Lydenberg, John, "Nature Myth in Faulkner's *The Bear*", *American Literature*, XXIV (March 1952), pp. 62-72.
Lytle, Andrew Nelson, "The Son of Man: He Will Prevail", *Sewanee Review*, LXIII (Winter 1955), pp. 114-37.
McClennan, Joshua, "William Faulkner and Christian Complacency", *Papers of the Michigan Academy of Science, Arts, and Letters*, XLI, pp. 315-32.
McCole, C. J., "William Faulkner: Cretins, Coffin-worms, and Cruelty", *Lucifer at Large* (New York, 1937).
Magne, Claude-Edmonde, *L'Age du Roman Americain* (Paris, 1948).
Malin, Irving, *William Faulkner, An Interpretation* (Stanford, Calif., 1953).
Malraux, André, "A Preface for Faulkner's *Sanctuary*", *Yale French Studies*, X (Fall 1952), pp. 92-94.
Marcus, Steven, "Snopes Revisited", *Partisan Review*, XXIV, 3 (Summer 1957), pp. 432-44.
Marvin, John R., "*Pylon:* The Definition of Sacrifice", *Faulkner Studies*, I (Summer 1952), pp. 20-23.
Millgate, Michael, *William Faulkner* (New York, 1961).
Miner, Ward L., "Faulkner and Christ's Crucifixion", *New Mexico Quarterly*, LVII (1956), pp. 260-69.
——, *The World of William Faulkner* (Chapel Hill, 1952).
Monteiro, George, "Initiation and the Moral Sense in Faulkner's *Sanctuary*", *Modern Language Notes*, LXXIII (November 1958), pp. 500-04.
Morris, Wright, "The Violent Land: Some Observations on the Faulkner Country", *Magazine of Art*, XLV (March 1952), pp. 99-103.
Moses, W. R., "The Unity of *The Wild Palms*", *Modern Fiction Studies*, II (Autumn 1956), pp. 125-31.
——, "Where History Crosses Myth: Another Reading of *The Bear*", *Accent*, XIII (Winter 1953), pp. 21-33.
O'Connor, William Van, *The Tangled Fire of William Faulkner* (Minneapolis, 1954).
O'Donnell, George Marion, "Faulkner's Mythology", *Kenyon Review*, I (Summer 1939), pp. 285-99.
Pearson, Norman Holmes, "Lena Grove", *Shenandoah*, III (Spring 1952), pp. 3-7.

182   BIBLIOGRAPHY

Perry, Bradley, "A Selected Bibliography of Critical Works on William Faulkner", *University of Kansas City Review*, XVIII (Winter 1951), pp. 159-64.

Peyre, Henri, *The Contemporary French Novel* (New York, 1955).

Podhoretz, Norman, "William Faulkner and the Problem of War", *Commentary*, XVIII September 1954), pp. 227-32.

Poirier, William, " 'Strange Gods' in Jefferson, Mississippi: Analysis of *Absalom, Absalom!*", *Two Decades of Criticism*, ed. Frederick T. Hoffman and Olga W. Vickery (East Lansing, 1951).

Powell, Sumner C., "William Faulkner Celebrates Easter, 1928", *Perspective*, II (Summer 1949), pp. 195-218.

Pritchett, V. S., "Time Frozen", *Partisan Review*, XXI (September-October 1954), pp. 557-61.

Rabi, "Faulkner and the Exiled Generation", *Two Decades of Criticism*, ed. Frederick J. Hoffman and Olga W. Vickery (East Lansing, 1951).

Ransom, John Crowe, "William Faulkner: An Impression", *Harvard Advocate*, CXXXV (November 1951), p. 17.

Reiner, Margrit, "The Fictional American Woman", *Masses and Mainstream*, VI (June 1952), pp. 1-10.

Rice, Philip Blair, "Faulkner's Crucifixion", *Kenyon Review*, XVI (Autumn 1954), pp. 661-70.

Robb, Mary Cooper, *William Faulkner: An Estimate of His Contribution to the Modern American Novel* (Pittsburgh, 1957).

Roth, Russell, "The Centaur and the Pear Tree", *Western Review*, XVI (Spring 1952), pp. 199-205.

Rourke, Constance, *American Humor* (New York, 1931).

Ryan, Marjorie, "The Shakespearean Symbolism in *The Sound and the Fury*", *Faulkner Studies*, II (Autumn 1953), pp. 40-44.

Sandeen, Ernest, "William Faulkner: His Legend and His Fable", *Review of Politics*, XVIII (January 1956), pp. 47-68.

Sartre, Jean-Paul, "American Novelists in French Eyes", *Atlantic*, CLXXVIII (August 1946), pp. 114-18.

——, *Literary and Philosophical Essays* (London, 1955).

——, "Time in Faulkner: *The Sound and the Fury*", *Two Decades of Criticism*, ed. Frederick J. Hoffman and Olga W. Vickery (East Lansing, 1951).

Schwartz, Delmore, "The Fiction of William Faulkner", *Southern Review*, VII (Summer 1941), pp. 145-60.

Sherwood, John C., "The Traditional Element in Faulkner", *Faulkner Studies*, III (Summer-Autumn 1954), pp. 17-23.

Slatoff, Walter J., *Quest for Failure: A Study of William Faulkner* (New York, 1960).

Smith, Henry Naish, "William Faulkner and Reality", *Faulkner Studies*, II (Summer 1953), pp. 17-19.

Starke, Aubrey, "An American Comedy: An Introduction to a Bibliography of William Faulkner", *Colophon*, Part XIX (1934).

Stavrou, C. N., "William Faulkner's Apologia: Some Notes on *A Fable*", *Colorado Quarterly*, III (Spring 1955), pp. 432-439.

Stewart, Randall, "Hawthorne and Faulkner", *College English*, XVII (February 1956), pp. 258-62.

Stonesifer, Richard J., "Faulkner's *Old Man* in the Classroom", *College English*, XVIII (February 1956), pp. 254-57.

Sullivan, Walter L., "Southern Novelists and the Civil War", *The Southern Renascence*, eds. Louis D. Rubin, Jr. and Robert D. Jacobs (Baltimore, 1953).

Swiggart, Peter, *The Art of Faulkner's Novels* (Austin, Texas, 1963).

——, "Moral and Temporal Order in *The Sound and the Fury*", *Sewanee Review*, CXI (Spring 1953), pp. 221-37.

——, "Time in Faulkner's Novels", *Modern Fiction Studies*, I (May 1955), pp. 25-29.

Thompson, Lawrance, "Mirror Analogues in *The Sound and The Fury*", *English Institute Essays* (New York, 1952).

——, *William Faulkner: An Introduction and Interpretation* (New York, 1963).

Tritschler, Donald, "The Unity of Faulkner's Shaping Vision", *Modern Fiction Studies*, V, 4 (Winter 1959-1960), pp. 337-43.

Vickery, John B., "William Faulkner and Sir Philip Sidney", *Modern Language Notes*, LXX (1950), pp. 349-50.

Vickery, Olga Westland, "*As I Lay Dying*", *Perspective*, III (Autumn 1950), pp. 179-91.

——, "Gavin Stevens: From Rhetoric to Dialectic", *Faulkner Studies*, II (Spring 1953), pp. 1-4.

——, *The Novels of William Faulkner* (Baton Rouge, 1959).

——, "*The Sound and the Fury*: A Study in Perspective", *PMLA*, LXIX (December 1954), pp. 1017-37.

Wagenknecht, Edward, *Cavalcade of the American Novel* (New York, 1952).

Waggoner, Hyatt, *William Faulkner: From Jefferson to the World* (Lexington, 1959).

Wagner, Geoffrey, "Faulkner's Contemporary Passion Play", *Twentieth Century*, CLVI (December 1954), pp. 527-38.

Warren, Robert Penn, "Cowley's Faulkner", *New Republic*, CXV (August 12, 1946), pp. 176-80.

——, *Selected Essays* (New York, 1958).

——, "The Snopes World", *Kenyon Review*, III (1941), pp. 253-57.

Wasserstrom, William, *Heiress of All the Ages* (Minneapolis, 1959).

West, Ray B., Jr., "Hemingway and Faulkner", *The Short Story in America 1900-1950* (Chicago, 1951).

——, "William Faulkner: Artist and Moralist", *Western Review*, XVI (Winter 1952), pp. 162-67.

Wilson, Edmund, "William Faulkner's Reply to the Civil-Rights Program", *Classics and Commercials* (New York, 1950).

Wirth, Louis, "Urbanism as a Way of Life", *Reader in Urban Sociology*, ed. Paul K. Hatt and Albert J. Reiss, Jr. (Illinois, 1951).

Zink, Karl E., "Faulkner's Garden: Woman and the Immemorial Earth", *Modern Fiction Studies*, II (Autumn 1956), pp. 139-49.

Zink, Karl E., "Flux and the Frozen Moment: The Imagery of Stasis in
Faulkner's Prose", *PMLA*, LXXI (June 1956), pp. 285-301.
——, "William Faulkner: Form as Experience", *South Atlantic Quarterly*,
LIII (July 1954), pp. 384-403.

INDEX

STUDIES IN AMERICAN LITERATURE

1. JOHN BERNSTEIN: *Pacifism and Rebellion in the Writings of Herman Melville*. 1964. 232 pp.   ƒ 25.—

2. KARL F. KNIGHT: *The Poetry of John Crowe Ransom: A Study of Diction, Metaphor, and Symbol*. 1964. 133 pp.   ƒ 14.50

3. KENT G. GALLAGHER: *The Foreigner in Early American Drama*. A Study in Attitudes. 1966. 206 pp., Cloth.   ƒ 24.—

4. PAUL T. NOLAN: *Three Plays by J. W. (Capt. Jack) Crawford: An Experiment in Myth-Making*. 1966. 287 pp., portrait.   ƒ 30.—

5. NORMAN J. FEDDER: *The Influence of D. H. Lawrence on Tennessee Williams*. 1966. 131 pp. Cloth.   ƒ 18.—

6. LEONARD GREENBAUM: *The Hound & Horn: The History of a Literary Quarterly*. 1966. 275 pp. 2 plates.   ƒ 30.—

10. EDWARD M. HOLMES: *Faulkner's Twice-Told Tales: His Re-Use of his Material*. 1966. 118 pp.   ƒ 19.—

MOUTON & CO · PUBLISHERS · THE HAGUE